EMPOWERED TO LIVE FREE

SIAFU MEN'S CONFERENCE 2016

Rev. Dr. Don L. Davis

The Urban Ministry Institute, *a ministry of* World Impact, Inc.

NO RESERVES RETREAT REGRETS

TUMI Press
3701 East Thirteenth Street North
Wichita, Kansas 67208

No Reserves, No Retreat, No Regrets: SIAFU Men's Conference 2016

The Urban Ministry Institute
3701 East 13th Street North
Wichita, KS 67208

ISBN: 978-1-62932-712-9

Published by TUMI Press
A division of World Impact, Inc.

The Urban Ministry Institute is a ministry of World Impact, Inc.

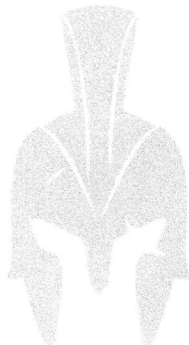

We dedicate this booklet to those

Soldiers of Christ in the Cities of the World

who serve Christ in places that are hard and unfriendly,
who don't hesitate to run toward the sound of the fight,
who have surrendered all they are and all they have to Christ,
who wage war against the flesh, the world, and the devil every day,
all for the sake of pleasing him who has
called them out of darkness
into his marvelous light.

For these fighters, who never run and never quit,
we dedicate this reflection and teaching.

May God grant to each one of them
the power to endure and to engage the enemy
until the victory for Christ has been won.

Stay awake, stand firm in your faith, be brave, be strong.

~ 1 Corinthians 16.13

"My name is Gladiator!"

Commodus: Your fame is well deserved, Spaniard. I don't think there's ever been a gladiator to match you. As for this young man, he insists you are Hector reborn. Or was it Hercules? Why doesn't the hero reveal himself and tell us all your real name? You do have a name.

Maximus: My name is Gladiator. [turns away from Commodus]

Commodus: How dare you show your back to me! Slave, you will remove your helmet and tell me your name.

Maximus: [removes helmet and turns around to face Commodus] My name is Maximus Decimus Meridius, commander of the Armies of the North, General of the Felix Legions and loyal servant to the TRUE emperor, Marcus Aurelius. Father to a murdered son, husband to a murdered wife. And I will have my vengeance, in this life or the next.

[Commodus trembles in disbelief.]

"The general who became a slave. The slave who became a gladiator. The gladiator who defied an emperor."

Commodus: The general who became a slave. The slave who became a gladiator. The gladiator who defied an emperor. Striking story! But now, the people want to know how the story ends. Only a famous death will do. And what could be more glorious than to challenge the Emperor himself in the great arena?

Maximus: You would fight me?

Commodus: Why not? Do you think I am afraid?

Maximus: I think you've been afraid *all your life.*

"If we stay together, we survive!"

Cassius: On this day, we reach back to hallowed antiquity, to bring you a recreation of the second fall of the mighty Carthage! . . . On the barren plain of Zama, there stood the invincible armies of the barbarian Hannibal. Ferocious mercenaries and warriors from all brute nations, bent on merciless destruction, conquest. Your emperor is pleased to give you the barbarian horde!
[Crowd cheers]

Maximus: [while Cassius continues his introduction] Anyone here been in the army? [an unknown gladiator responds yes and tells Maximus he served under his command at Vindobona]

Maximus: You can help me. Whatever comes out of these gates, we've got a better chance of survival if we work together. Do you understand? If we stay together we survive.

"No reserves, no retreat, no regrets."

"Yet how few have made the impact that young William Borden did, as he inspired his generation and the generations to come with a sterling example of a life lived as a flame of fire for the cause of Jesus Christ. When they looked into his Bible they found three powerful phrases written at different times in his life. While he was in school, having made his decision to forsake a comfortable life of wealth and ease in the U. S. he had written, 'No reserves.' After graduating from Yale, with many offers of important positions coming to him, he wrote, 'No retreat.' And below these two phrases, written shortly before he died, were the amazing words, 'No regrets.'"

A long time ago there was a woman who was also considered wasteful. She broke an extremely expensive alabaster box of oil, worth nearly a year's wages, and poured it over the Master's head. When some objected to the "waste" our Lord refused to condemn her, saying that wherever the gospel was preached this woman's act of total devotion would be shared as a memorial to her. William Borden was of the same spirit. The Lord Jesus, who gave His precious life and blood for us, deserves our best.

And it is never a waste when we give it.

~ Taylor, *Borden of Yale*

Jesus of Nazareth: No Reserves, No Retreat, No Regrets

Have this mind among yourselves, which is yours in Christ Jesus,
who, though he was in the form of God,
did not count equality with God a thing to be grasped,
but emptied himself, by taking the form of a servant,
being born in the likeness of men.

And being found in human form,
he humbled himself by becoming obedient to the point of death,
even death on a cross.

Therefore God has highly exalted him
and bestowed on him the name that is above every name,
so that at the name of Jesus every knee should bow,
in heaven and on earth and under the earth,
and every tongue confess that Jesus Christ is Lord,
to the glory of God the Father.

– Philippians 2.5-11

Table of Contents

No Reserves, No Retreat, No Regrets: Introduction 11

No Reserves, No Retreat, No Regrets: Theme Song 12

Session Outlines

Session 1
No Reserves: Surrender All to Christ, Without Conditions. 15

Session 2
No Retreat: Stand Your Ground for Christ, No Matter What 35

Session 3
No Regrets: Lose Everything for What Really Counts,
Without Disappointment 55

Appendix

Appendix 1
The Story of God: Our Sacred Roots 75

Appendix 2
Incorporation into the People of the Story:
Steps of Discipling Others into the Story of God 76

Appendix 3
The Theology of Christus Victor 77

Appendix 4
Christus Victor:
An Integrated Vision for the Christian Life and Witness 78

Appendix 5
Ladd's View of Time 79

Appendix 6
Jesus of Nazareth: The Presence of the Future 80

Appendix 7
The Cost of Discipleship 81

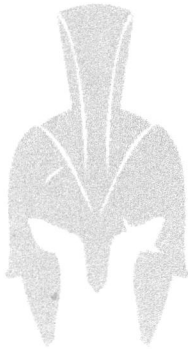

Appendix 8
Substitute Centers to a Christ-Centered Vision: Goods and
Effects Which Our Culture Substitutes as the Ultimate Concern. . . 82

Appendix 9
The Importance of Discipline 83

Appendix 10
Understanding Leadership as Representation:
The Six Stages of Formal Proxy 85

Appendix 11
Steps to Equipping Others 86

Appendix 12
An Outline for a Vision for Discipleship:
"Let's Give Jesus Christ Our Best and All" 88

Appendix 13
Living as an *Oikos* Ambassador 93

Appendix 14
The *Oikos* Factor: Spheres of Relationship and Influence 94

Appendix 15
Elements of an *Oikos* 95

Appendix 16
Paul's Team Members: Companions, Laborers, and Fellow Workers . 96

Appendix 17
Getting a Firm Grasp of Scripture 99

Appendix 18
Spiritual Growth Diagram 100

Appendix 19
Personal Growth vs. Body Life: Connections 101

Appendix 20
Shoe Manufacturing Plant 102

Appendix 21
Fit to Represent: Multiplying Disciples of the Kingdom of God . . 103

Appendix 22
From Deep Ignorance to Credible Witness 104

Appendix 23
Laws of Sowing and Reaping 105

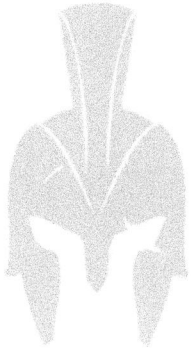

Appendix 24
Roles of Effective Discipling 106

Appendix 25
The Power of Multiplication: 2 Timothy 2.2 Discipleship Diagram . 107

Appendix 26
The Hump 108

Appendix 27
Principles of Spiritual Growth 109

Appendix 28
A Spiritual Warfare Bibliography 110

No Reserves, No Retreat, No Regrets: Introduction

The theme for our 2016 SIAFU Men's Conference is *No Reserves, No Retreat, No Regrets*. Jesus of Nazareth, the living and risen Lord of all, is calling all people to a life of sacrifice and discipleship. He offers his kingdom blessings to all, even to those whom the enemy has enslaved to sin and bondage that no mere mortal could ever overcome. The Son of God was sent from heaven into this enemy-occupied territory in order to defeat Satan and his foes, to release the captives and set the prisoners free – to empower us to live free from the shackles and miseries of the devil's cruelty. Now, as the victorious Champion of God who defeated the powers through his sinless life and saving death, Jesus calls us to join his "great campaign of sabotage," a campaign to take back our cities for God.

We will follow the storyline of *Gladiator*, a gripping movie tale of a general who became a slave, a slave who became a gladiator, and a gladiator that defied an emperor. As modern-day soldiers of Jesus Christ, we are called to a life of freedom, to a warfare that is constant, and to a struggle that will end in victory for those who endure. Christ's call is a call to a discipleship that holds no reserves (giving full surrender to the Lord), that knows no retreat (holds its ground in the worst of battles), and owns no regrets (fights bravely till the end, no matter what). Come, and join the ranks of Christ's men of honor, the brave and faithful who know what it takes to advance the Kingdom of God in our world today.

> "What we do in life echoes in eternity."
>
> ~ Maximus

As soldiers of Jesus, we trust in him alone. We hold nothing in reserve, never shrink back from any fight, and have no regrets for serving him as our Commander and Lord.

No Reserves, No Retreat, No Regrets

Don L. Davis (Lyrics) Bobby Gilmer (Music)
Written for the attendees of the SIAFU Men's Conference 2016

(Chorus)
No reserves, no retreat, no regrets
Army strong, we respond to the threat
Gospel truth we display and confess
No reserves, no retreat, no regrets

(Verse)
All we have we will give to the Lord
All we need we will get from his word
All we got we lay down for his praise
All we want is to lift up his name

(Bridge)
We won't hold nothing back
We will press the attack
We won't give in to fear
We'll make doubt disappear
No reserves, no retreat
Won't accept no defeat
No more fear, no regrets
Crowns of life we collect

EMPOWERED TO LIVE FREE
SIAFU Men's Conference 2016

NO RESERVES RETREAT REGRETS

Stay awake, stand firm in your faith, be brave, be strong.
~ 1 Corinthians 16.13 (CEB)

SESSION OUTLINES

EMPOWERED TO LIVE FREE
SIAFU Men's Conference 2016

NO RESERVES RETREAT REGRETS

Stay awake, stand firm in your faith, be brave, be strong.
~ 1 Corinthians 16.13 (CEB)

Session 1

No Reserves

Surrender All to Christ, Without Conditions

Rev. Dr. Don L. Davis

Session 1

No Reserves

Surrender All to Christ, Without Conditions

Our Confession of Allegiance

We confess Jesus of Nazareth as Lord, our Savior, God's only Son, and our Master.

We believe that he died to redeem us, that he has risen from the dead, and that now he sits at God's right hand as Lord and King.

Therefore, we cling to no reserves: all we are and all we have we surrender to him, without condition.

And we will never retreat: we will stand our ground in the daily struggle, by his grace, no matter what.

Finally, we hold no regrets: we do not yield to disappointment, for we know that what we gain is greater than anything in this world we might lose.

As soldiers of Jesus Christ, we will depend on him to help us represent his Kingdom, please him in our relationships and conduct, and make disciples wherever we go.

To him be the glory, forever. Amen!

Session 1

No Reserves

Surrender All to Christ, without Conditions

Rev. Dr. Don L. Davis

Get Ready – You're in the Fight of Your Life

The essence of all really great accomplishments is acting wisely and wholly in that moment that taxes you greatly. Every struggle that matters presents you with only a few options, and whatever you choose, you will reap a host of consequences, based on the choice you make. God has called every Christian to fight, to be a soldier, to engage the enemy with the armor that he himself has provided to all of us (Eph. 6.10-18). Victory demands that we consider the options, make our choice, and follow through with obedience and perseverance till the end. Thankfully, we do not have to fight alone. The weapons of our warfare are designed to provide us with the power to overcome (2 Cor. 10.3-5).

- **You can give up.** When faced with some outward challenge, you can simply surrender to the fight; raise the white flag, and give yourself over to the enemy's mercies (Gal. 6.7-10).

- **You can give in.** The sheer weight and pressure of the test can cause you inwardly to just give in to temptation; this kind of surrender is not from an enemy without, but due to your own issues within (1 Cor. 13.7; 2 Tim. 3.12; Acts 14.22).

- **You can give all you got to the Lord.** Inspired by the example of Christ and his bond servants in the Scriptures and life, we can surrender all that we are and all we have to God, that he might do in and through us whatever he pleases (4.7; 1 Pet. 5.8-9).

As warriors of the Kingdom, we commit ourselves without condition to Jesus Christ, as both the Savior and Lord of all our lives.

As soldiers of Jesus Christ, called to Kingdom advance, we possess . . .

- *No Reserves: we surrender all to Christ, without conditions*
- **No Retreat:** we stand our ground for Christ, no matter what
- **No Regrets:** we lose everything for what really counts, without disappointment

I. Set the Stage: Why do men try to run things themselves, even when they have already made a mess of everything?

The American Sickness of Being Exceptional But Not Deep

The "show business," which is so incorporated into our view of Christian work today, has caused us to drift far from Our Lord's conception of discipleship. It is instilled in us to think that we have to do exceptional things for God; we have not. We have to be exceptional in ordinary things, to be holy in mean streets, among mean people, surrounded by sordid sinners. That is not learned in five minutes.

~ Oswald Chambers

What does it take for a man to finally admit that he cannot live a full, satisfying, and meaningful life without the Lord?

God respects the will of a man. Although he could make every man respond to him with faith and commitment, he chooses to allow each man to determine his own direction. A man is a special part of his creation given the right to say yes or no to the offer of God Almighty!

List some reasons why you think men refuse to turn their lives over to the Lord.

1.

2.

3.

4.

5.

II. Tell the Story: Joshua, the servant of the Lord, yielded everything he had to the Lord. He clung to *no reserves*.

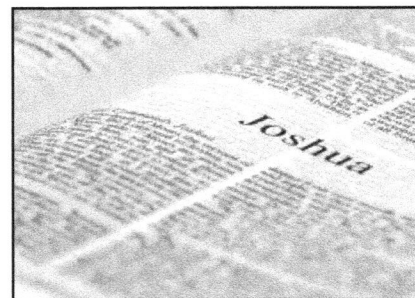

    A. **Joshua and Caleb, young bucks: early on Joshua showed a wholehearted devotion to the Lord.**

        1. He was drafted by Moses to be his apprentice and "chief of staff."

            a. First mentioned at the battle with Amalek, Exod. 17.9-10 – So Moses said to Joshua, "Choose for us men, and go out and fight with Amalek. Tomorrow I will stand on the top of the hill with the staff of God in my hand." [10] So Joshua did as Moses told him, and fought with Amalek, while Moses, Aaron, and Hur went up to the top of the hill.

            b. Became the servant of Moses, his "assistant", Exod. 24.12-13 – The LORD said to Moses, "Come up to me on the mountain and wait there, that I may give you the tablets of stone, with the law and the commandment, which I have written for their instruction." [13] So Moses rose with his assistant Joshua, and Moses went up into the mountain of God.

2. The Lord's commissioning and recognition of Joshua, Num. 27.18-23 – So the LORD said to Moses, "Take Joshua the son of Nun, a man in whom is the Spirit, and lay your hand on him. [19] Make him stand before Eleazar the priest and all the congregation, and you shall commission him in their sight. [20] You shall invest him with some of your authority, that all the congregation of the people of Israel may obey. [21] And he shall stand before Eleazar the priest, who shall inquire for him by the judgment of the Urim before the LORD. At his word they shall go out, and at his word they shall come in, both he and all the people of Israel with him, the whole congregation." [22] And Moses did as the LORD commanded him. He took Joshua and made him stand before Eleazar the priest and the whole congregation, [23] and he laid his hands on him and commissioned him as the LORD directed through Moses.

3. Was chosen by Moses to go with Caleb and ten others to spy out the land (took 40 days to check it out), Num. 13-14

4. *The ten doubted but Caleb and Joshua believed: "They will be bread for us (i.e., "We gonna eat them up!").*

   a. Num. 13.30-33 – But Caleb quieted the people before Moses and said, "Let us go up at once and occupy it, for we are well able to overcome it." [31] Then the men who had gone up with him said, "We are not able to go up against the people, for they are stronger than we are." [32] So they brought to the people of Israel a bad report of the land that they had spied out, saying, "The land, through which we have gone to spy it out, is a land that devours its inhabitants, and all the people that we saw in it are of great height. [33] And there we saw the Nephilim (the sons of Anak, who come from the Nephilim), and we seemed to ourselves like grasshoppers, and so we seemed to them."

b. Num. 14.6-10 – And Joshua the son of Nun and Caleb the son of Jephunneh, who were among those who had spied out the land, tore their clothes [7] and said to all the congregation of the people of Israel, "The land, which we passed through to spy it out, is an exceedingly good land. [8] If the LORD delights in us, he will bring us into this land and give it to us, a land that flows with milk and honey. [9] Only do not rebel against the LORD. And do not fear the people of the land, for they are bread for us. Their protection is removed from them, and the LORD is with us; do not fear them." [10] Then all the congregation said to stone them with stones. But the glory of the LORD appeared at the tent of meeting to all the people of Israel.

5. Joshua from the start determined to never sell out or give in; he was not a newbie, but rather a seasoned, tried, and proven young leader who sold out early to the Lord, even before the fight! His victories are won by faith, not by his own might, 1 John 5.4 – For everyone who has been born of God overcomes the world. And this is the victory that has overcome the world – our faith.

B. **Joshua surrendered all to the Lord to serve as leader of God's people after Moses' death, Josh. 1.1-9.**

1. Moses is dead; don't cling to the old days, take your place as God's man, Josh. 1.1-2 – After the death of Moses the servant of the LORD, the LORD said to Joshua the son of Nun, Moses' assistant, [2] "Moses my servant is dead. Now therefore arise, go over this Jordan, you and all this people, into the land that I am giving to them, to the people of Israel.

2. For the next phase of my will, you are my choice, and I'll be with you, Josh. 1.3-5 – Every place that the sole of your foot will tread upon I have given to you, just as I promised to Moses. [4] From the wilderness and this Lebanon as far as the great river, the river Euphrates, all the land of the Hittites to the Great Sea toward the going down of the sun shall be your territory. [5] No man shall be able to stand before you all the days of your life. Just as I was with Moses, so I will be with you. I will not leave you or forsake you.

3. My goal is ambitious, everywhere you stand, that I will give you. Be strong and courageous, and meditate upon and obey my Word, Josh. 1.6-8 – Be strong and courageous, for you shall cause this people to inherit the land that I swore to their fathers to give them. [7] Only be strong and very courageous, being careful to do according to all the law that Moses my servant commanded you. Do not turn from it to the right hand or to the left, that you may have good success wherever you go. [8] This Book of the Law shall not depart from your mouth, but you shall meditate on it day and night, so that you may be careful to do according to all that is written in it. For then you will make your way prosperous, and then you will have good success.

C. **God encouraged Joshua's heart to surrender with a constant refrain and charge: "Be strong and courageous!"**

1. Joshua is told to be "strong and courageous" numerous times.

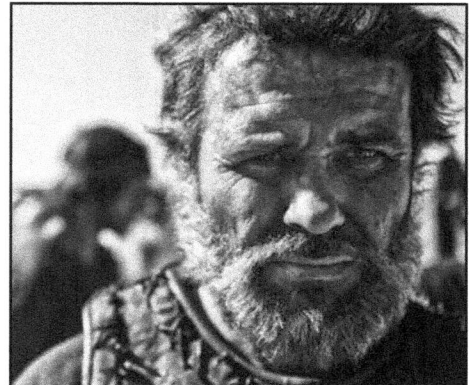

2. Moses tells him this, Deut. 31.6 – Be strong and courageous. Do not fear or be in dread of them, for it is the LORD your God who goes with you. He will not leave you or forsake you.

3. The people tell Joshua to be strong and courageous, Josh. 1.18 – Whoever rebels against your commandment and disobeys your words, whatever you command him, shall be put to death. Only be strong and courageous."

4. God repeatedly tells Joshua to be strong and courageous.

    a. Deut. 31.23 – And the LORD commissioned Joshua the son of Nun and said, "Be strong and courageous, for you shall bring the people of Israel into the land that I swore to give them. I will be with you."

    b. Josh. 1.6-7 – Be strong and courageous, for you shall cause this people to inherit the land that I swore to their fathers to give them. [7] Only be strong and very courageous, being careful to do according to all the law that Moses my servant commanded you. Do not turn from it to the right hand or to the left, that you may have good success wherever you go.

    c. Josh. 1.9 – Have I not commanded you? Be strong and courageous. Do not be frightened, and do not be dismayed, for the LORD your God is with you wherever you go.

D. God guaranteed Joshua's surrender with divine intervention: the Commander of the Lord's Armies, Josh. 5-6.27.

1. Joshua does not go by himself; God provides his own commander to lead the way, Josh. 5.13-15 – When Joshua was by Jericho, he lifted up his eyes and looked, and behold, a man was standing before him with his drawn sword in his hand. And

Joshua went to him and said to him, "Are you for us, or for our adversaries?" [14] And he said, "No; but I am the commander of the army of the LORD. Now I have come." And Joshua fell on his face to the earth and worshiped and said to him, "What does my lord say to his servant?" [15] And the commander of the LORD's army said to Joshua, "Take off your sandals from your feet, for the place where you are standing is holy." And Joshua did so.

2. God's unique protocols of preparation for his warriors: sacrifice (thanksgiving to God), circumcision (cutting away of all fleshly help), and purity (recognizing the Lord is in our midst, Josh. 2-7), cf. Josh. 5.2-5 – At that time the LORD said to Joshua, "Make flint knives and circumcise the sons of Israel a second time." [3] So Joshua made flint knives and circumcised the sons of Israel at Gibeath-haaraloth. [4] And this is the reason why Joshua circumcised them: all the males of the people who came out of Egypt, all the men of war, had died in the wilderness on the way after they had come out of Egypt. [5] Though all the people who came out had been circumcised, yet all the people who were born on the way in the wilderness after they had come out of Egypt had not been circumcised.

3. Rahab, the prostitute, protects the scouts and saves her own life, and sees the lives of her family spared, Josh. 2.8-13.

4. The wall will fall down at Jericho and victory will be won (sore warriors and cycling around Jericho on foot, with trumpet blast – an unlikely war strategy! (Josh. 6), cf. Josh. 6.15-19 – On the seventh day they rose early, at the dawn of day, and marched around the city in the same manner seven times. It was only on that day that they marched around the city seven times. [16] And at the seventh time, when the

priests had blown the trumpets, Joshua said to the people, "Shout, for the LORD has given you the city. [17] And the city and all that is within it shall be devoted to the LORD for destruction. Only Rahab the prostitute and all who are with her in her house shall live, because she hid the messengers whom we sent. [18] But you, keep yourselves from the things devoted to destruction, lest when you have devoted them you take any of the devoted things and make the camp of Israel a thing for destruction and bring trouble upon it. [19] But all silver and gold, and every vessel of bronze and iron, are holy to the LORD; they shall go into the treasury of the LORD."

5. God will stop the sun, and rain huge hailstones down upon the enemy (Josh. 10). (For those who surrender, the battle belongs to the Lord!, e.g., 1 Sam. 17.45-47 – Then David said to the Philistine, "You come to me with a sword and with a spear and with a javelin, but I come to you in the name of the LORD of hosts, the God of the armies of Israel, whom you have defied. 46 This day the LORD will deliver you into my hand, and I will strike you down and cut off your head. And I will give the dead bodies of the host of the Philistines this day to the birds of the air and to the wild beasts of the earth, that all the earth may know that there is a God in Israel, 47 and that all this assembly may know that the LORD saves not with sword and spear. For the battle is the LORD's, and he will give you into our hand.")

E. **Joshua's surrender to God was fortified by God's command to meditate on and obey his Word, Josh. 1.8.**

1. God commanded Joshua to be strong and very courageous, being careful to do according to all the law that God had given to the people through Moses, Josh. 1.7-8 – Only be strong and very courageous, being careful to do according to all the law that Moses my servant commanded you. Do not

turn from it to the right hand or to the left, that you may have good success wherever you go. [8] This Book of the Law shall not depart from your mouth, but you shall meditate on it day and night, so that you may be careful to do according to all that is written in it. For then you will make your way prosperous, and then you will have good success.

2. The assurance of absolute surrender?: Josh. 1.9 – Have I not commanded you? Be strong and courageous. Do not be frightened, and do not be dismayed, for the LORD your God is with you wherever you go."

3. *The mission and task God has for a person's life can only be accomplished when that person turns over their life to God without condition*, Deut. 11.24-25 – Every place on which the sole of your foot treads shall be yours. Your territory shall be from the wilderness to the Lebanon and from the River, the river Euphrates, to the western sea.[25] No one shall be able to stand against you. The LORD your God will lay the fear of you and the dread of you on all the land that you shall tread, as he promised you.

The battle for your surrender is also the battle for your life.

Let God have your life today – all of it that's left.

Let God have your life; He can do more with it than you can.

~ Dwight L. Moody

The man or woman who is wholly or joyously surrendered to Christ can't make a wrong choice – any choice will be the right one.

~ A. W. Tozer

You become stronger only when you become weaker. When you surrender your will to God, you discover the resources to do what God requires.

~ Erwin Lutzer

III. Hammer It Home: Hold back no reserves. Surrender all to Christ without condition.

A car is made to run on gasoline, and it would not run properly on anything else. Now **God designed the human machine to run on Himself** [emphasis mine]. He Himself is the fuel our spirits were designed to burn, or the food our spirits were designed to feed on. There is no other. That is why it is just no good asking God to make us happy in our own way without bothering about religion. God cannot give us a happiness and peace apart from Himself, because it is not there. There is no such thing.

~ C. S. Lewis. *Mere Christianity.*
from *Notable Harbour In-Depth Studies, Joshua, WordSearch Digital Resources.*

A. **The Key Principle.** *Jesus is calling all people everywhere to discipleship, to come to him, receive salvation, and be equipped as his warrior,* Matt. 16.24-27; cf. Luke 13.1-5.

1. We are saved by grace through faith, and that not of ourselves; the price of salvation is free – simple belief and clinging to God's salvation offer given in his Son, John 3.16; 5.24; 6.35; Eph. 2.8-10.

2. What do you think this means? – "Grace is *absolutely free* but it will *cost you everything*" (Dietrich Bonhoeffer).

3. Surrender to Christ is about defeating his cosmic enemy. Jesus' offer of surrender is a part of his plan to defeat the powers that rebel against God and infest our world – liberating you is a part God's liberation of everything, i.e., nature, systems, animals, humankind, all creation. *To lose you is to lose part of his creation, and he ain't having that!*, 1 John 3.8; Luke 14.25-33; Matt. 6.33.

B. **The Key Illustration:** Do you function *Canteen style* or *Nozzle style*?

1. *Canteen style* operates on the basis of a limited, prescribed amount that can be used up, and then needs to be refilled. (See Jer. 2.13 – for my people have committed two evils: they have forsaken me, the fountain of living waters, and hewed out cisterns for themselves, broken cisterns that can hold no water.) *Nozzle style*, however, is about tapping into God's unlimited power source, abiding in it, letting it flow through you. It is about hooking up to the source of power and having continuous divine supply. (Zech. 4.6 – Then he said to me, "This is the word of the LORD to Zerubbabel: Not by might, nor by power, but by my Spirit, says the LORD of hosts.)

2. *Canteen style* has to carefully measure out in particular units its contents in order to make it last; *Nozzle style* does not worry about the amount of the contents, but only that the

nozzle is connected to the proper source. (Eph. 5.15-19 – Look carefully then how you walk, not as unwise but as wise, [16] making the best use of the time, because the days are evil. [17] Therefore do not be foolish, but understand what the will of the Lord is. [18] And do not get drunk with wine, for that is debauchery, but be filled with the Spirit.)

3. *Canteen style* has to constantly be refilled because it can only hold so much, making it hard to share with others; *Nozzle style* knows that once it is properly connected to a source, it can direct its content to whomever or wherever it is most needed. (John 7.37-39 – On the last day of the feast, the great day, Jesus stood up and cried out, "If anyone thirsts, let him come to me and drink. [38] Whoever believes in me, as the Scripture has said, 'Out of his heart will flow rivers of living water.'" [39] Now this he said about the Spirit, whom those who believed in him were to receive, for as yet the Spirit had not been given, because Jesus was not yet glorified.)

C. **The Key Implications**

1. *Jesus surrendered all that he had to the Lord in coming to the earth as God's Suffering Servant, Phil. 2.5-6.*

2. *All who have been used have surrendered themselves to God* without qualification.

   a. Their *time*: Matt. 10.38-39 – And whoever does not take his cross and follow me is not worthy of me. [39] Whoever finds his life will lose it, and whoever loses his life for my sake will find it.

   b. Their *talent*: Rev. 3.15-17 – "'I know your works: you are neither cold nor hot. Would that you were either cold or hot! [16] So, because you are lukewarm, and neither hot nor cold, I will spit you out of my mouth. [17] For you say, I am rich, I have prospered, and I need nothing, not realizing that you are wretched, pitiable, poor, blind, and naked.

  c. Their *treasure*: Luke 5.11 – And when they had brought their boats to land, they left everything and followed him; Luke 14.33 – So therefore, any one of you who does not renounce all that he has cannot be my disciple.

 3. *Those who hold on to the things of this life and this world* do not experience the fullness of Jesus' liberation, freedom, and blessing, John 12.24-25 – Truly, truly, I say to you, unless a grain of wheat falls into the earth and dies, it remains alone; but if it dies, it bears much fruit.[25] Whoever loves his life loses it, and whoever hates his life in this world will keep it for eternal life.

D. **The Key Connections**

 1. *Receive God's offer of salvation – confess Jesus as Lord*, Job 23.13 – But he is unchangeable, and who can turn him back? What he desires, that he does.

 2. *Surrender your life and future into the hands of the Lord*, as if you were risen from the grave to live only for him, Prov. 19.21 – Many are the plans in the mind of a man, but it is the purpose of the LORD that will stand.

 3. *Start today to live as an obedient disciple of Jesus*, doing the next thing you know that he wants of you, today, Heb. 3.7-12 – Therefore, as the Holy Spirit says, "Today, if you hear his voice, [8] do not harden your hearts as in the rebellion, on the day of testing in the wilderness, [9] where your fathers put me to the test and saw my works for forty years. [10] Therefore I was provoked with that generation, and said, 'They always go astray in their heart; they have not known my ways.'[11] As I swore in my wrath, 'They shall not enter my rest.'" [12] Take care, brothers, lest there be in any of you an evil, unbelieving heart, leading you to fall away from the living God.

What does it mean to "Follow Jesus"?

Those who aren't following Jesus aren't his followers. It's that simple. Followers follow, and those who don't follow aren't followers. To follow Jesus means to follow Jesus into a society where justice rules, where love shapes everything. To follow Jesus means to take up his dream and work for it.

~ Scot McKnight. *One Life: Jesus Calls, We Follow*

Jesus-shaped spirituality hears Jesus say "believe and repent," but the call that resonates most closely in the heart of a disciple is "follow me." The command to follow requires that we take a daily journey in the company of other students. It demands that we be lifelong learners and that we commit to constant growth in spiritual maturity. Discipleship is a call to me, but it is a journey of "we."

~ Michael Spencer.
Mere Churchianity: Finding Your Way Back to Jesus-Shaped Spirituality.

Everything in Scripture is either preparation for the Gospel, presentation of the Gospel, or participation in the Gospel.

~ Dave Harvey

Die, or remain alone . . .

John 12.24-25 – Truly, truly, I say to you, unless a grain of wheat falls into the earth and dies, it remains alone; but if it dies, it bears much fruit. [25] Whoever loves his life loses it, and whoever hates his life in this world will keep it for eternal life.

Welcome to the War

Every Christian is a walking battlefield. Every believer carries deep within himself a terrible conflict. And most of us will gravitate to anything that will help us win the battle. Call it the battle between the flesh and the spirit. Call it the quest for the victorious Christian life. Call it what you want. But it's a flat-out-knock-down-drag-out war. And when it's over, you want to be among those who are still standing. The principles of war are taught in military academies all over the world. In most ways, spiritual warfare is no different than physical warfare. Every soldier who expects to not only survive but win must understand and employ these principles in his own daily battles "against the powers of this dark world and against the spiritual forces of evil in the heavenly realms" (Ephesians 6.12b NIV).

~ Stu Webber. *Spirit Warriors*.
Sisters, OR: Multnomah Publishers, 2001, p. 16.

As soldiers of Jesus Christ, called to Kingdom advance, we possess . . .

- *No Reserves: we surrender all to Christ, without conditions*
- **No Retreat**: we stand our ground for Christ, no matter what
- **No Regrets**: we lose everything for what really counts, without disappointment

Session 1 Notes

Session 1 Notes

EMPOWERED TO LIVE FREE
SIAFU Men's Conference 2016

NO
RESERVES
RETREAT
REGRETS

Stay awake, stand firm in your faith, be brave, be strong.
~ 1 Corinthians 16.13 (CEB)

Session 2
No Retreat

Stand Your Ground for Christ, No Matter What

Rev. Dr. Don L. Davis

Session 2

No Retreat

Stand Your Ground for Christ, No Matter What

Our Confession of Allegiance

We confess Jesus of Nazareth as Lord, our Savior, God's only Son, and our Master.

We believe that he died to redeem us, that he has risen from the dead, and that now he sits at God's right hand as Lord and King.

Therefore, we cling to no reserves: all we are and all we have we surrender to him, without condition.

And we will never retreat: we will stand our ground in the daily struggle, by his grace, no matter what.

Finally, we hold no regrets: we do not yield to disappointment, for we know that what we gain is greater than anything in this world we might lose.

As soldiers of Jesus Christ, we will depend on him to help us represent his Kingdom, please him in our relationships and conduct, and make disciples wherever we go.

To him be the glory, forever. Amen!

Session 2

No Retreat

Stand Your Ground for Christ, No Matter What

Rev. Dr. Don L. Davis

Our Greatest Weakness: Giving Up Too Soon Before Victory

Our greatest weakness lies in giving up. The most certain way to succeed is always to try just one more time.

~ Thomas A. Edison

Giving up smoking is the easiest thing in the world. I know because I've done it thousands of times.

~ Mark Twain

We all have dreams. But in order to make dreams come into reality, it takes an awful lot of determination, dedication, self-discipline, and effort.

~ Jesse Owens

Now to him who is able to do far more abundantly than all that we ask or think, according to the power at work within us, to him be glory in the church and in Christ Jesus throughout all generations, forever and ever. Amen.

~ Paul, Ephesians 3.20-21

We must learn that retreat is unacceptable.
To be a soldier of Christ is to ever engage in battle against the enemy – the world, the flesh, and the devil.

As soldiers of Jesus Christ, called to Kingdom advance, we possess . . .

- **No Reserves**: we surrender all to Christ, without conditions
- *No Retreat: we stand our ground for Christ, no matter what*
- **No Regrets**: we lose everything for what really counts, without disappointment

I. Set the Stage: Why does it seem so easy to quit and give up sometimes, and really hard to stand up against the enemy?

First Signs of New Life: Learning to Take Sides

One of the consequences of sin is that it makes the sinner pity himself instead of causing him to turn to God. One of the first signs of new life is that the individual takes sides with God against himself.

~ Donald Grey Barnhouse

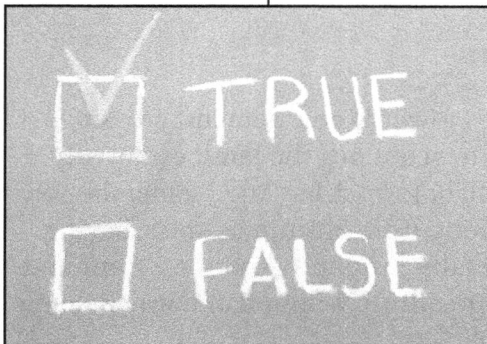

Answer why you think some Christians are prone to retreat.

T or F 1. I am most likely to give in to sin when I neglect spending time with my fellow soldiers in Christ.

T or F 2. Everyone who lives godly in Christ will certainly be tempted to quit.

T or F 3. The time the enemy is most likely to attack us is when we are broken and hurting, when we are humbled and yielded before the Lord.

T or F 4. The Word of God in the heart is the best remedy in fighting the temptation to give up in the midst of a fierce spiritual battle.

T or F 5. Fellowship with others can't guarantee victory; if you win, you win for yourself, and if you lose, you lose for yourself.

T or F 6. Fervent, constant prayer is God's antidote against giving in to fear, to retreat.

T or F 7. You can always say no to any temptation or attack the devil designs against us; we do not have to accept his lies in anything or in any matter.

II. Tell the Story: Joshua never retreated or backed down, even in the face of constant trials, setbacks, and obstacles.

A. **Joshua was built for battle**: regardless of the odds or the situation, he was always on the attack.

1. Joshua with Caleb were on the attack even before they engaged the enemy: chosen as spies at Kadesh-Barnea, Num. 13-14.

2. Joshua moved God's forces towards engagement, crossing the Jordan, sending spies to scout out the land, eventually hooking them up with Rahab, Josh. 2.1 – And Joshua the son of Nun sent two men secretly from Shittim as spies, saying, "Go, view the land, especially Jericho." And they went and came into the house of a prostitute whose name was Rahab and lodged there.

3. Joshua prepared for war by allowing his guys to be circumcised before the battle, and then walking around Jericho in a silent parade before God delivered the city to him, sparing Rahab!, Josh. 5-6.

4. Joshua wins Jericho by the shout of the trumpets and the cry of the soldiers!, Josh. 6, cf. Josh. 6.20-25 – So the people shouted, and the trumpets were blown. As soon as the people heard the sound of the trumpet, the people shouted a great shout, and the wall fell down flat, so that the people went up into the city, every man straight before him,

and they captured the city. [21] Then they devoted all in the city to destruction, both men and women, young and old, oxen, sheep, and donkeys, with the edge of the sword. [22] But to the two men who had spied out the land, Joshua said, "Go into the prostitute's house and bring out from there the woman and all who belong to her, as you swore to her." [23] So the young men who had been spies went in and brought out Rahab and her father and mother and brothers and all who belonged to her. And they brought all her relatives and put them outside the camp of Israel. [24] And they burned the city with fire, and everything in it. Only the silver and gold, and the vessels of bronze and of iron, they put into the treasury of the house of the LORD. [25] But Rahab the prostitute and her father's household and all who belonged to her, Joshua saved alive. And she has lived in Israel to this day, because she hid the messengers whom Joshua sent to spy out Jericho.

B. **Joshua faced down defeat and setback with perseverance and heart:** even in the face of horrible defeat and deception, Joshua stayed in the fight.

1. At the horrible defeat and set back at Ai with Achan, Joshua cries out to God, finds out the source of the problem, and deals with it thoroughly, Josh. 7.

   a. Josh. 7.4-9 – So about three thousand men went up there from the people. And they fled before the men of Ai, [5] and the men of Ai killed about thirty-six of their men and chased them before the gate as far as Shebarim and struck them at the descent. And the hearts of the people melted and became as water. [6] Then Joshua tore his clothes and fell to the earth on his face before the ark of the LORD until the evening, he and the elders of Israel. And they put dust on their heads. [7] And Joshua said, "Alas, O Lord GOD, why have you brought this people over the Jordan at all, to give us into the hands of the Amorites, to

destroy us? Would that we had been content to dwell beyond the Jordan! [8] O Lord, what can I say, when Israel has turned their backs before their enemies! [9] For the Canaanites and all the inhabitants of the land will hear of it and will surround us and cut off our name from the earth. And what will you do for your great name?"

b. Josh. 7.19-21 – Then Joshua said to Achan, "My son, give glory to the LORD God of Israel and give praise to him. And tell me now what you have done; do not hide it from me." [20] And Achan answered Joshua, "Truly I have sinned against the LORD God of Israel, and this is what I did: [21] when I saw among the spoil a beautiful cloak from Shinar, and 200 shekels of silver, and a bar of gold weighing 50 shekels, then I coveted them and took them. And see, they are hidden in the earth inside my tent, with the silver underneath."

c. Josh. 7.24-26 – And Joshua and all Israel with him took Achan the son of Zerah, and the silver and the cloak and the bar of gold, and his sons and daughters and his oxen and donkeys and sheep and his tent and all that he had. And they brought them up to the Valley of Achor. [25] And Joshua said, "Why did you bring trouble on us? The LORD brings trouble on you today." And all Israel stoned him with stones. They burned them with fire and stoned them with stones. [26] And they raised over him a great heap of stones that remains to this day. Then the LORD turned from his burning anger. Therefore, to this day the name of that place is called the Valley of Achor.

2. Though deceived by the Gibeonites, Joshua honors his treaty and whips the enemy throughout the entire southern area of warfare, Josh. 9-10.

a. The Gibeon deception and the treaty with them 9.1-26

b. Keeping his treaty with Gibeon, Josh defeats the Canaanite coalition army, 10.9-15.

c. God makes us victorious even after setbacks: he stepped in and defeated the Canaanite alliance with divine power: with hailstones, making the sun stand still, 10.9-15.

d. Joshua effectively wiped out the rest of the southern area resistance of the Canaanite nations, 10.16-42.

C. **Joshua fights till the end with valor and focus:** Joshua engaged the fight with courage and strength, and showed no respect for either the spoils or the weaponry of the enemy, Josh. 11.1-15.

1. He defeated the Canaanite kings and their cities, 11.1-5.

2. He hamstrung the enemy's horses and burned their chariots, Josh. 11.6-9.

3. He captured Hazor and its king with the sword, devoted everything to destruction as Moses had given command ("they did not leave any who breathed"), and took all the spoil for plunder, 11.10-16.

4. Joshua had bucket loads of heavenly mojo: *he simply did not play around when it came to accomplishing God's will:* Josh. 10.22-27 – Then Joshua said, "Open the mouth of the cave and bring those five kings out to me from the cave." [23] And they did so, and brought those five kings out to him from the cave, the king of Jerusalem, the king of Hebron, the king of Jarmuth, the king of Lachish, and the king of Eglon. [24] And when they brought those kings out to Joshua, Joshua summoned all the men of Israel and said to the chiefs of the men of war who had gone with him, "Come near; put your feet on the necks of these kings." Then they came near

and put their feet on their necks. [25] And Joshua said to them, "Do not be afraid or dismayed; be strong and courageous. For thus the LORD will do to all your enemies against whom you fight." [26] And afterward Joshua struck them and put them to death, and he hanged them on five trees. And they hung on the trees until evening. [27] But at the time of the going down of the sun, Joshua commanded, and they took them down from the trees and threw them into the cave where they had hidden themselves, and they set large stones against the mouth of the cave, which remain to this very day.

5. Christus Victor – To Christ be the victory!: Joshua's wrap up summary, Josh. 11.16-12.24

6. "Waged war for a long time" against the Canaanites; never quit, never shrunk back, always persevered in the fight, cf. 11.18

D. **Speed-bumps in your past don't matter; it's not where you've been, but your level of surrender: Achan versus Rahab.**

1. The just will live by faith: Rahab (Josh. 2) with Achan (Josh. 7). Rahab's faith: Josh. 2.8-13 – Before the men lay down, she came up to them on the roof [9] and said to the men, "I know that the LORD has given you the land, and that the fear of you has fallen upon us, and that all the inhabitants of the land melt away before you. [10] For we have heard how the LORD dried up the water of the Red Sea before you when you came out of Egypt, and what you did to the two kings of the Amorites who were beyond the Jordan, to Sihon and Og, whom you devoted to destruction. [11] And as soon as we heard it, our hearts melted, and there was no spirit left in any man because of you, for the LORD your God, he is God in the heavens above and on the earth beneath. [12] Now then, please swear to me by the LORD that, as I have dealt kindly with you, you also will deal kindly with

my father's house, and give me a sure sign [13] that you will save alive my father and mother, my brothers and sisters, and all who belong to them, and deliver our lives from death."

Rahab (Josh. 2)	Achan (Josh. 7)
A disfavored woman	An honored man in Israel
A Canaanite, who walks by faith	An Israelite, but doesn't fear God
A prostitute	A family head among God's people
Should have died, but lived	Should have lived, but perished
Was the savior of her family clan	Doomed his own family clan
Survived, along with her goods	Perished, along with his stuff
She alone of her nation remained	He alone of his nation was judged
Hid the spies	Hid the loot
Covered up the guys on the roof	Buried his stolen treasure in the dirt
She obeyed God's indirect word	He disobeyed God's clear command
She lives, with the Israelites	He died, with the Canaanites
She walked by faith	He walked by sight
Possessed a deep fear of God	Possessed a fear of getting caught
Joined the ranks of God's favored folk	Joined the ranks of the dishonorable
Received the blessings of faith	Received the judgments of dishonor

III. Hammer It Home: In every spiritual fight, never shrink back or never retreat. Stand your ground for Christ, no matter what.

He was the perfect soldier: he went where you sent him, and stayed where you put him, and had no idea of his own to keep him from doing exactly what you told him.

~ Dashiell Hammett

A. **The Key Principle.** *True disciples of Jesus trust and obey his Word, and refuse to shrink back or retreat regardless of the situation.* Matt. 16.24-27; cf. Luke 13.1-5.

1. As disciples of the Lord Jesus, we are to embrace his word, clinging to its promise and following its command, without wavering or change. Through it we know the truth, and the truth sets us free, John 8.31-32 – So Jesus said to the Jews who had believed him, "If you abide in my word, you are truly my disciples, [32] and you will know the truth, and the truth will set you free."

2. Jesus stood his ground throughout his earthly ministry, and we are called to do the same, Heb. 12.1-3 – Therefore, since we are surrounded by so great a cloud of witnesses, let us also lay aside every weight, and sin which clings so closely, and let us run with endurance the race that is set before us, [2] looking to Jesus, the founder and perfecter of our faith, who for the joy that was set before him endured the cross, despising the shame, and is seated at the right hand of the throne of God. [3] *Consider him who endured from sinners such hostility against himself, so that you may not grow weary or fainthearted.*

3. Even though we will face tribulation in this world (e.g., hurts, struggles, disappointments, opposition, persecution, trials), we overcome in the name of Jesus!

a. 1 John 5.4 – For everyone who has been born of God overcomes the world. And this is the victory that has overcome the world – our faith.

b. 1 Cor. 15.57 – But thanks be to God, who gives us the victory through our Lord Jesus Christ.

c. John 16.33 – I have said these things to you, that in me you may have peace. In the world you will have tribulation. But take heart; I have overcome the world."

4. We should never quit or give up to discouragement or opposition from the enemy, 1 Pet. 5.8-9 – Be sober-minded; be watchful. Your adversary the devil prowls around like a roaring lion, seeking someone to devour. [9] Resist him, firm in your faith, knowing that the same kinds of suffering are being experienced by your brotherhood throughout the world.

B. **The Key Illustration:** Do you function in your Christian walk *Wave style* or *Spike style*?

1. *Wave style* operates on the basis of being subject to other outward forces which determines where it winds up. It is easily impacted and moved. *Spike style* is about being driven into a fixed point and refusing to move – period. (Cf. Isa. 54.2 – Enlarge the place of your tent, and let the curtains of your habitations be stretched out; do not hold back; lengthen your cords and strengthen your stakes.)

2. *Wave style* is completely vulnerable to whatever wind gusts are blowing; it is virtually impossible to navigate on waves that are being tossed around. (Cf. Eph. 4.14-15 – so that we may no longer be children, tossed to and fro by the waves and carried about by every wind of doctrine, by human cunning, by craftiness in deceitful schemes. [15] Rather, speaking the truth in love, we are to grow up in every way into him who is the head, into Christ.) *Spike style*, however, does not move or bend. Its glory is to stay where it is put and never turn loose of its spot, for anything! (Ps. 125.1 – Those who trust in the LORD are like Mount Zion, which cannot be moved, but abides forever.)

Let God have your life today – all of it that's left.

Let God have your life; He can do more with it than you can.

~ Dwight L. Moody

The man or woman who is wholly or joyously surrendered to Christ can't make a wrong choice – any choice will be the right one.

~ A. W. Tozer

You become stronger only when you become weaker. When you surrender your will to God, you discover the resources to do what God requires.

~ Erwin Lutzer

---

3. *Wave style* is always being affected by stuff, and is therefore unstable, doubting, flitting, floating, exhausted from being blown around. (James 1.6-8 – But let him ask in faith, with no doubting, for the one who doubts is like a wave of the sea that is driven and tossed by the wind. [7] For that person must not suppose that he will receive anything from the Lord; [8] he is a double-minded man, unstable in all his ways.) *Spike style* is firmly planted and refuses to turn back; it would rather be broken than turned around. ("I ain't go let nobody turn me 'round, turn me 'round, turn me 'round . . .")

C. **The Key Implications:** No one who trusts and obeys Christ need to fear shrinking back; they need never retreat, regardless of what they face.

1. Those who trust in the Lord and his strength will not be ashamed.

   a. Ps. 25.1-3 – To you, O LORD, I lift up my soul. [2] O my God, in you I trust; let me not be put to shame; let not my enemies exult over me. [3] Indeed, none who wait for you shall be put to shame; they shall be ashamed who are wantonly treacherous.

   b. Ps. 31.1-4 – In you, O LORD, do I take refuge; let me never be put to shame; in your righteousness deliver me! [2] Incline your ear to me; rescue me speedily! Be a rock of refuge for me, a strong fortress to save me! [3] For you are my rock and my fortress; and for your name's sake you lead me and guide me; [4] you take me out of the net they have hidden for me, for you are my refuge.

   c. Ps. 71.1-3 – In you, O LORD, do I take refuge; let me never be put to shame! [2] In your righteousness deliver me and rescue me; incline your ear to me, and save me! [3] Be to me a rock of refuge, to which I may continually come; you have given the command to save me, for you are my rock and my fortress.

2. Regardless of what lies ahead for you, you need never fear; you will not be moved!

   a. Ps. 112.6-8 – For the righteous will never be moved; he will be remembered forever. [7] He is not afraid of bad news; his heart is firm, trusting in the LORD. [8] His heart is steady; he will not be afraid, until he looks in triumph on his adversaries.

b. Ps. 125.1 – Those who trust in the LORD are like Mount Zion, which cannot be moved, but abides forever.

c. Isa. 26.3 – You keep him in perfect peace whose mind is stayed on you, because he trusts in you.

3. God's wisdom and counsel are a sure foundation; you will not slip or falter if you follow it, to the end.

a. Rom. 9.33 – as it is written, "Behold, I am laying in Zion a stone of stumbling, and a rock of offense; and whoever believes in him will not be put to shame."

b. Rom. 10.11 – For the Scripture says, "Everyone who believes in him will not be put to shame."

c. 1 Pet. 2.6 – For it stands in Scripture: "Behold, I am laying in Zion a stone, a cornerstone chosen and precious, and whoever believes in him will not be put to shame."

D. **The Key Connections**

1. *Don't be surprised at trouble and setback, but rather, dig in, strap your armor on, and hold your ground – it is always too soon to quit.*

a. Acts 14.21-22 – When they had preached the gospel to that city and had made many disciples, they returned to Lystra and to Iconium and to Antioch, [22] strengthening the souls of the disciples, encouraging them to continue in the faith, and saying that through many tribulations we must enter the kingdom of God.

b. John 16.33 – I have said these things to you, that in me you may have peace. In the world you will have tribulation. But take heart; I have overcome the world.

c. 1 Thess. 3.3-4 – . . . that no one be moved by these afflictions. For you yourselves know that we are destined for this. [4] For when we were with you, we kept telling you beforehand that we were to suffer affliction, just as it has come to pass, and just as you know.

d. Gal. 6.7-9 – Do not be deceived: God is not mocked, for whatever one sows, that will he also reap. [8] For the one who sows to his own flesh will from the flesh reap corruption, but the one who sows to the Spirit will from the Spirit reap eternal life. [9] And let us not grow weary of doing good, for in due season we will reap, if we do not give up.

2. *Don't try to win the entire war in a single fight in one day; stand your ground right here, right now, today.*

a. Matt. 6.34 (MSG) – "Give your entire attention to what God is doing right now, and don't get worked up about what may or may not happen tomorrow. God will help you deal with whatever hard things come up when the time comes.

b. James 4.13-14 – Come now, you who say, "Today or tomorrow we will go into such and such a town and spend a year there and trade and make a profit" – [14] yet you do not know what tomorrow will bring. What is your life? For you are a mist that appears for a little time and then vanishes.

c. Ps. 39.6 – Surely a man goes about as a shadow! Surely for nothing they are in turmoil; man heaps up wealth and does not know who will gather!

d. Eccles. 3.14 – I perceived that whatever God does endures forever; nothing can be added to it, nor anything taken from it. God has done it, so that people fear before him.

e. Luke 12.25-26 – And which of you by being anxious can add a single hour to his span of life? [26] If then you are not able to do as small a thing as that, why are you anxious about the rest?

f. Lam. 3.22-24 – The steadfast love of the LORD never ceases; his mercies never come to an end; [23] they are new every morning; great is your faithfulness. [24] "The LORD is my portion," says my soul, "therefore I will hope in him."

3. *Talk back to the enemy by telling yourself the truth, and praying to the Lord – over and over and over again.*

a. 2 Cor. 4.13-15 – Since we have the same spirit of faith according to what has been written, "I believed, and so I spoke," we also believe, and so we also speak, [14] knowing that he who raised the Lord Jesus will raise us also with Jesus and bring us with you into his presence. [15] For it is all for your sake, so that as grace extends to more and more people it may increase thanksgiving, to the glory of God.

John 8.31-32 – So Jesus said to the Jews who had believed him, "If you abide in my word, you are truly my disciples, [32] and you will know the truth, and the truth will set you free."

b. Luke 18.1-8, cf. v. 1 – And he told them a parable to the effect that they ought always to pray and not lose heart.

c. Rom. 12.1-2 – I appeal to you therefore, brothers, by the mercies of God, to present your bodies as a living sacrifice, holy and acceptable to God, which is your spiritual worship. [2] Do not be conformed to this world, but be transformed by the renewal of your mind, that by testing you may discern what is the will of God, what is good and acceptable and perfect.

d. Luke 21.36 – But stay awake at all times, praying that you may have strength to escape all these things that are going to take place, and to stand before the Son of Man.

When Tempted to Quit, Remember What Jesus Did for Us

May nothing entice me till I happily make my way to Jesus Christ! Fire, cross, struggles with wild beasts, wrenching of bones, mangling of limbs – let them come to me, provided only I make my way to Jesus Christ.

~ Ignatius of Antioch

Consider him who endured from sinners such hostility against himself, so that you may not grow weary or fainthearted.

~ Hebrews 12.3

A disciple is not above his teacher, nor a servant above his master. [25] It is enough for the disciple to be like his teacher, and the servant like his master. If they have called the master of the house Beelzebul, how much more will they malign those of his household.

~ Matthew 10.24-25

We Live Because Jesus Refused to Quit—He Gave His All for Us

For you know the grace of our Lord Jesus Christ, that though he was rich, yet for your sake he became poor, so that you by his poverty might become rich.

~ 2 Corinthians 8.9

Love Will Never Let You Fail

For those who love, nothing is too difficult, especially when it is done for the love of our Lord Jesus Christ.

~ Ignatius of Antioch, 72.

As soldiers of Jesus Christ, called to Kingdom advance, we possess . . .

- **No Reserves:** we surrender all to Christ, without conditions
- *No Retreat: we stand our ground for Christ, no matter what*
- **No Regrets:** we lose everything for what really counts, without disappointment

Session 2 Notes

EMPOWERED TO LIVE FREE

SIAFU Men's Conference 2016

NO RESERVES RETREAT REGRETS

Stay awake, stand firm in your faith, be brave, be strong.
~ 1 Corinthians 16.13 (CEB)

Session 3

No Regrets

Lose Everything for What Really Counts, Without Disappointment

Rev. Dr. Don L. Davis

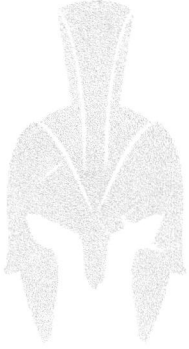

No Regrets

Lose Everything for What Really Counts, Without Disappointment

Our Confession of Allegiance

We confess Jesus of Nazareth as Lord, our Savior, God's only Son, and our Master.

We believe that he died to redeem us, that he has risen from the dead, and that now he sits at God's right hand as Lord and King.

Therefore, we cling to no reserves: all we are and all we have we surrender to him, without condition.

And we will never retreat: we will stand our ground in the daily struggle, by his grace, no matter what.

Finally, we hold no regrets: we do not yield to disappointment, for we know that what we gain is greater than anything in this world we might lose.

As soldiers of Jesus Christ, we will depend on him to help us represent his Kingdom, please him in our relationships and conduct, and make disciples wherever we go.

To him be the glory, forever. Amen!

Session 3

No Regrets

Lose Everything for What Really Counts, Without Disappointment

Rev. Dr. Don L. Davis

What Famous Folk Have Said about Having Regrets

The only time you really live fully is from thirty to sixty. The young are slaves to dreams; the old servants of regrets. Only the middle-aged have all their five senses in the keeping of their wits.

~ Theodore Roosevelt

Regrets are the natural property of grey hairs.

~ Charles Dickens

You can't be in the public eye without making mistakes and having some regrets and having people analyze everything you do.

~ Sheryl Crow

Make the most of your regrets; never smother your sorrow, but tend and cherish it till it comes to have a separate and integral interest. To regret deeply is to live afresh.

~ Henry David Thoreau

You can always say, "I wish I had landed that triple flip better, or I wish I didn't fall." They're not regrets, just mistakes.

~ Michelle Kwan

What You Can Always Do: Accepting the Power of Change

You can't go back and change the beginning, but you can start where you are and change the ending.

~ C.S. Lewis

Regret is the enemy's attempt to get us to believe that our past mistakes label us effectively as a "screw up," that our current condition is pretty much "jacked up," and that our future will inevitably be "messed up" because of who we are and what we have done. He uses his entire arsenal of lies to convince us that we are a disappointment, that we have basically missed out on an even a better opportunity at a full life in Christ.

Don't you dare believe it.

As soldiers of Jesus Christ, called to Kingdom advance, we possess . . .

- **No Reserves:** we surrender all to Christ, without conditions
- **No Retreat:** we stand our ground for Christ, no matter what
- *No Regrets: we lose everything for what really counts, without disappointment*

I. Set the Stage: Why do we suffer from the pain and shame of regret?

Looking Back, Looking Over: Defining Regret

The general meaning of the term *regret* is to feel sorrow or remorse for an act, fault, or disappointment usually beyond one's control or power to change, correct or repair. To regret is to feel the pain of living with the reality that you could have done things differently, become more than what you have become, accomplished more, done less harm, and fulfilled dreams and tasks that now are no longer attainable. To regret is to be haunted by the thinking that flows from the phrase, "If I had only . . . , then things would have really turned out differently." Regret is an expression of the distress caused by being deeply convinced that a past act or situation must affect everything you will ever do, and that you simply can no nothing about it. Don't believe it.

F_LL IN THE BL_NK

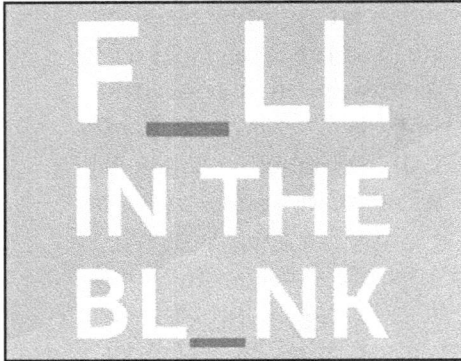

Complete the following statements on how you feel about your past and its impact on your present life, and future.

1. "Of all the things I wish I would have done, I think the biggest thing is _____."

2. "If I could change one thing in the last five years of my life, I would go back and _____."

3. "When I look back on my life, I think the one great opportunity that I missed for a better life _____."

4. "The times I am most ashamed of what I have done in the past are usually _____."

5. "When I think about my past, and how I think it is going to affect my future, I usually think that _____."

These questions appear to be okay, but they can easily foster much suffering and shame about a believer's past behaviors and situations. How might the enemy use this kind of thinking to poison a believer's spirit?

II. Tell the Story: Joshua fulfilled his mission and completed his task without excuse, complaint, or deviation. He had no regrets.

A. **Joshua had no regrets in that he thoroughly defeated the Canaanites through his trust and obedience to God's divine power and direction:** When it came to the will of the Lord, Joshua did not play around, hesitate, or vacillate. He was all business for the Lord.

1. Joshua conquered Canaan in the Central campaign including Jericho and Ai (chaps. 6-8), the Southern campaign (including the alliance and defense of the Gibeonites (chaps. 9-10), and the Northen campaign (chaps. 11.1-15).

2. The book of Joshua reviews Joshua's victories, both the areas whipped and the kings defeated (chaps. 11-12), and the division of land among the tribes (chaps. 13-21), with special attention given to Caleb's inheritance in chapter 14.

3. Joshua resolves a border dispute among the tribes in chapter 22, and gives a final challenge to the leaders and to the people in chapters 23 and 24 respectively.

4. The entire book of Joshua reveals one major thing about his character: Joshua don't play!

   a. His chest would have been filled with medals from the numerous battles fought and won in the Lord's name and power.

   b. They conquered significant land (11.16-12.24), and 31 kings (chap. 12)!

Be Free of Guilt, Regret, and Shame in Christ Alone

You don't have to live with guilt, regret, or shame anymore. Too many people are stuck with memories from their past that they can't get over. Either you've been hurt and have resentment or you've hurt someone else and you have guilt. God doesn't want you to carry that heavy baggage throughout your life. He wants you to be free. That's one reason God gave us the Bible. He uses his Word to eradicate our guilt.

~ Rick Warren

5. This absolute warfare was in fulfillment of God's command to Moses.

a. He made war with the kings "a long time," Josh. 11.18-20 – Joshua made war a long time with all those kings. [19] There was not a city that made peace with the people of Israel except the Hivites, the inhabitants of Gibeon. They took them all in battle. [20] For it was the LORD's doing to harden their hearts that they should come against Israel in battle, in order that they should be devoted to destruction and should receive no mercy but be destroyed, just as the LORD commanded Moses.

b. Joshua was thorough; not a piece or part of God's will did he carry out, but the whole, Josh. 11.23 – So Joshua took the whole land, according to all that the LORD had spoken to Moses. And Joshua gave it for an inheritance to Israel according to their tribal allotments. And the land had rest from war.

B. **Joshua had no regrets seen in his blessing of Caleb, his partner in fierce zeal for the will of God:** both Joshua and Caleb, the original spies who believed, finished their job! (Cf. Josh. 14)

1. Joshua's companion, Caleb, reveals in his testimony that he lost nothing in his fighting spirit over 45 years!

Josh. 14.7-12 (ESV) – "I was forty years old when Moses the servant of the LORD sent me from Kadesh-barnea to spy out the land, and I brought him word again as it was in my heart. [8] But my brothers who went up with me made the heart of the people melt; yet I wholly followed the LORD my God. [9] And Moses swore on that day, saying, 'Surely the land on which your foot has trodden shall be an inheritance for you and your children forever, because you have wholly followed the LORD my God.' [10] And now, behold, the LORD has kept me alive, just as he said, these forty-five years since the time that the LORD spoke this word to Moses, while Israel walked in the wilderness. And now, behold, I am this day eighty-five years old. [11] I am still as strong today as I was in the day that Moses sent me; my strength now is as my strength was then, for war and for going and coming. [12] So now give me this hill country of which the LORD spoke on that day, for you heard on that day how the Anakim were there, with great fortified cities. It may be that the LORD will be with me, and I shall drive them out just as the LORD said."

2. Joshua blessed Caleb and gave Hebron for his inheritance, Josh. 14.13-15 – Then Joshua blessed him, and he gave Hebron to Caleb the son of Jephunneh for an inheritance. [14] Therefore Hebron became the inheritance of Caleb the son of Jephunneh the Kenizzite to this day, because he wholly followed the LORD, the God of Israel. [15] Now the name of Hebron formerly was Kiriath-arba. (Arba was the greatest man among the Anakim.) And the land had rest from war.

3. From the original call to the rest from the war, Joshua and Caleb did not play – they fulfilled God's will from A to Z!

   a. From the original report of the first spying of the land (even as the Lord promised them rest *four times* before they entered the land, e.g. chap. 1.15): Num. 13.30-33 – But Caleb quieted the people before Moses and said, "Let us go up at once and occupy it, for we are well able to overcome it." [31] Then the men who had gone up with him said, "We are not able to go up against the people, for they are stronger than we are." [32] So they brought to the people of Israel a bad report of the land that they had spied out, saying, "The land, through which we have gone to spy it out, is a land that devours its inhabitants, and all the people that we saw in it are of great height. [33] And there we saw the Nephilim (the sons of Anak, who come from the Nephilim), and we seemed to ourselves like grasshoppers, and so we seemed to them."

b. To the final fulfillment of the mission: Josh. 14.13-14 – Then Joshua blessed him, and he gave Hebron to Caleb the son of Jephunneh for an inheritance. [14] Therefore Hebron became the inheritance of Caleb the son of Jephunneh the Kenizzite to this day, because he wholly followed the LORD, the God of Israel.

4. Every promise God made to give them rest he fulfilled; Joshua didn't play because he knew that *God don't play!*

a. Josh. 11.23 – So Joshua took the whole land, according to all that the LORD had spoken to Moses. And Joshua gave it for an inheritance to Israel according to their tribal allotments. And the land had rest from war.

b. Josh. 14.15 – Now the name of Hebron formerly was Kiriath-arba. (Arba was the greatest man among the Anakim.) And the land had rest from war.

c. Josh. 21.44 – And the LORD gave them rest on every side just as he had sworn to their fathers. Not one of all their enemies had withstood them, for the LORD had given all their enemies into their hands.

d. Josh. 22.4 – And now the LORD your God has given rest to your brothers, as he promised them. Therefore turn and go to your tents in the land where your possession lies, which Moses the servant of the LORD gave you on the other side of the Jordan.

C. **Joshua had no regrets as revealed in his farewell exhortation and challenge to the leaders and people:** Joshua fought for as long as he needed to get the job done – no excuses, no complaints, no regrets, Josh. 23-24.

1. Joshua's lack of regret is revealed in Joshua's address to the elders, heads, judges, officers, and leaders, Josh. 23.

   a. God has fought for you in the past: Now old and advanced in years, he reminded them of what the Lord had done, Josh. 23.3 – And you have seen all that the LORD your God has done to all these nations for your sake, for it is the LORD your God who has fought for you.

   b. God will fight for you in the future: the same Lord who kept his promises up till now will continue to fulfill them in the future, Josh. 23.5 – The LORD your God will push them back before you and drive them out of your sight. And you shall possess their land, just as the LORD your God promised you.

2. Joshua gives the leaders three powerful exhortations, and one assurance.

   a. *Exhortation #1:* Be very strong to keep and to do all that is written in the Word of God, 23.6-7.

   b. *Exhortation #2:* Cling to the Lord your God who fights for you, 23.8-10.

   c. *Exhortation #3:* Love the Lord your God, and never turn back to human strength or false gods, 23.11-13.

d. *One blessed assurance:* God don't play!, Josh. 23.14-16 – "And now I am about to go the way of all the earth, and you know in your hearts and souls, all of you, that not one word has failed of all the good things that the LORD your God promised concerning you. All have come to pass for you; not one of them has failed. [15] But just as all the good things that the LORD your God promised concerning you have been fulfilled for you, so the LORD will bring upon you all the evil things, until he has destroyed you from off this good land that the LORD your God has given you, [16] if you transgress the covenant of the LORD your God, which he commanded you, and go and serve other gods and bow down to them. Then the anger of the LORD will be kindled against you, and you shall perish quickly from off the good land that he has given to you."

3. Joshua's lack of regret is also revealed in his address to the gathered tribes of Israel at Shechem, Josh. 24.

a. *You can only go forward by looking back:* Joshua recites and reviews a brief history of the Lord's gracious promise and work for the ancestors of his people, 24.2-13.

    (1) Abraham and their kin who dwelt on the other side of the flood, 24.2-4

    (2) God's great and majestic deliverance of their fathers and mothers from Egypt, 24.5-7

    (3) God's defeat of the Amorites (Sihon and Og's armies), and God's frustration of Balak and Balaam's blessing, 24.8-10

    (4) God's conquest of Canaan, 24.11-13

b. Joshua's threefold challenge to the people, 24.14-28

    (1) *Challenge #1:* Fear the Lord and serve him in sincerity and faithfulness, 14a.

(2) *Challenge #2:* Put away the gods that your fathers served, and serve the Lord, 14b.

(3) *Challenge #3:* Choose today whom you will serve, the Lord or other false gods (*this is the antidote for regret!*), 15a (notice Joshua's refusal to follow anyone but the Lord, v. 15, Joshua – And if it is evil in your eyes to serve the LORD, choose this day whom you will serve, whether the gods your fathers served in the region beyond the River, or the gods of the Amorites in whose land you dwell. But as for me and my house, we will serve the LORD.")

c. The people's response: "God is the one who rescued us, and we will serve the Lord!" vv. 16-18

d. Joshua's warning: "You're not going to be able to serve the LORD, because the Lord don't play; if you forsake him he will turn on you and do you harm. You are witnesses against yourselves that you have chosen the LORD to serve him."

4. Conclusion: Joshua made a covenant with the people that day, and put in place statutes and rules for them at Shechem, writing these words in the Book of the Law of God, 24.25-28.

D. The end of Joshua's ministry and journey, Josh. 24.29-33

1. Joshua the son of Nun, the servant of the LORD, died 110 years young, and Israel served the LORD all the days of Joshua, and the elders who outlived Joshua and who knew the work that the LORD did for Israel, 24.29-31.

2. Joseph's bones were buried at Shechem, and Eleazar, Aaron's son, was buried at Gibeah, 24.32-33.

God's Plea to You:
Don't Remember the Former Things – New Life Is Ahead

Remember not the former things, nor consider the things of old. Behold, I am doing a new thing; now it springs forth, do you not perceive it? I will make a way in the wilderness and rivers in the desert. The wild beasts will honor me, the jackals and the ostriches, for I give water in the wilderness, rivers in the desert, to give drink to my chosen people, the people whom I formed for myself that they might declare my praise.

~ Isaiah 43.18-21

III. Hammer It Home: We should receive forgiveness for our past, lose everything for the one thing that really matters – for Christ alone – and never regret it, not even for a moment.

Twenty years from now you will be more disappointed by the things you didn't do than by the ones you did do. So throw off the bowlines. Sail away from the safe harbor. Catch the trade winds in your sails. Explore. Dream. Discover.

~ Mark Twain

A. **The Key Principle.** *True disciples of Jesus follow him radically, sacrificing everything, knowing full well that nothing that they do for the Lord will be done in vain, 1 Cor. 15.58.*

1. We hold on to no reserves and never retreat because we are convinced that we will never regret it ever!, 1 Cor. 15.58 – Therefore, my beloved brothers, be steadfast, immovable, always abounding in the work of the Lord, knowing that in the Lord your labor is not in vain.

2. To play it safe is to play it wrong: "It may be hard for an egg to turn into a bird: it would be a jolly sight harder for it to learn to fly while remaining an egg. We are like eggs at present. And you cannot go on indefinitely being just an ordinary, decent egg. We must be hatched or go bad" (C. S. Lewis).

3. Don't be fooled: you only make your mark in this world by thinking of the implications of the world to come. "If you read history you will find that the Christians who did most for the present world were precisely those who thought most of the next. It is since Christians have largely ceased to think of the other world that they have become so ineffective in this [world]" (Ibid).

B. **The Key Illustration:** Are you currently living *Party Whistle style* or *Trumpet style*?

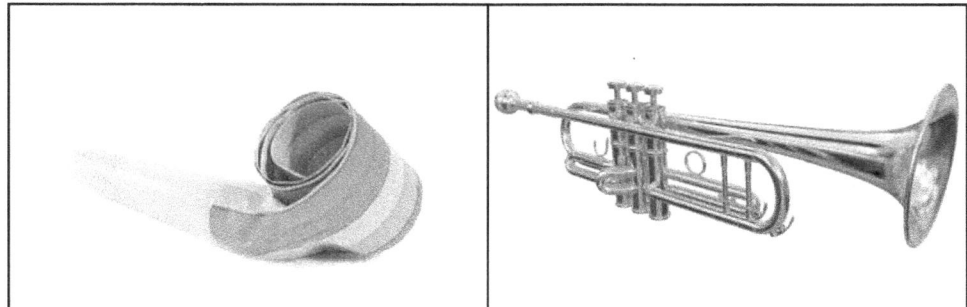

1. *Party whistle style* focuses on making lots of noise, even celebration sound, but in the end all it is, is noise, never a song. *Trumpet style* can be recognized to play songs of all kinds, even calling potential soldiers into formation for action.

2. *Party whistle style* doesn't care if it plays any given notes in any order. It only blows a single sound, with no melody or arrangement. *Trumpet style*, however, concentrates on making things clear so everyone knows what to do, how to act, and where to go, in the right place and time. (1 Cor. 14.7-8 – If even lifeless instruments, such as the flute or the harp, do not give distinct notes, how will anyone know what is played? [8] And if the bugle gives an indistinct sound, who will get ready for battle?)

3. *Party whistle style* usually only draws attention to itself, while *Trumpet style* plays the song that encourages the heart, mobilizes the troops, and lifts up the spirit. (Judg. 7.16-18 – And he divided the 300 men into three companies and put trumpets into the hands of all of them and empty jars, with torches inside the jars. [17] And he said to them, "Look at me, and do likewise. When I come to the outskirts of the camp, do as I do. 18 When I blow the trumpet, I and all who are with me, then blow the trumpets also on every side of all the camp and shout, 'For the LORD and for Gideon.'")

C. **The Key Implications:** Anyone who sacrifices for the sake of Christ and his Kingdom will receive much more than they offered, and never feel regret or remorse over it.

1. Those who offer all will receive 100 times more than they offered, along with the persecution that comes from serving Jesus!, Mark 10.25-30 – It is easier for a camel to go through the eye of a needle than for a rich person to enter the kingdom of God." [26] And they were exceedingly astonished, and said to him, "Then who can be saved?" [27] Jesus looked at them and said, "With man it is impossible, but not with God. For all things are possible with God." [28] Peter began to say to him, "See, we have left everything and followed you." [29] Jesus said, "Truly, I say to you, there is no one who has left house or brothers or sisters or mother or father or children or lands, for my sake and for the gospel, [30] who will not receive a hundredfold now in this time, houses and brothers and sisters and mothers and children and lands, with persecutions, and in the age to come eternal life.

2. Those who offer all may be tempted to live for the here and now, but their labor will never be in vain, not in this world or the one to come, Ps. 73.23-28 – Nevertheless, I am continually with you; you hold my right hand. [24] You guide me with your counsel, and afterward you will receive me to glory. [25] Whom have I in heaven but you? And there is nothing on earth that I desire besides you. [26] My flesh and my heart may fail, but God is the strength of my heart and my portion forever. [27] For behold, those who are far from you shall perish; you put an end to everyone who is unfaithful to you. [28] But for me it is good to be near God; I have made the Lord GOD my refuge, that I may tell of all your works.

3. Those who offer all experience God's rich provision and blessing in this life, provided they do not give up, Gal. 6.7-9 – Do not be deceived: God is not mocked, for whatever one sows, that will he also reap. [8] For the one who sows to his own flesh will from the flesh reap corruption, but the one who sows to the Spirit will from the Spirit reap eternal life. [9] And let us not grow weary of doing good, for in due season we will reap, if we do not give up.

D. **The Key Connections**

1. *Abound in the work of the Lord, just like you are going to be rewarded for it – for you are*, 1 Cor. 15.58 – Therefore, my beloved brothers, be steadfast, immovable, always abounding in the work of the Lord, knowing that in the Lord your labor is not in vain.

2. *Let the blood of Jesus clean your conscience over past mistakes, blunders, and sins. Live free of remorse, sorrow, guilt – and regret!*

a. Heb. 9.13-14 – For if the blood of goats and bulls, and the sprinkling of defiled persons with the ashes of a heifer, sanctify for the purification of the flesh, [14] how much more will the blood of Christ, who through the eternal Spirit offered himself without blemish to God, purify our conscience from dead works to serve the living God.

b. 1 John 1.8-10 – If we say we have no sin, we deceive ourselves, and the truth is not in us. [9] If we confess our sins, he is faithful and just to forgive us our sins and to cleanse us from all unrighteousness. [10] If we say we have not sinned, we make him a liar, and his word is not in us.

3. *Refuse to be enslaved by your past; strain forward to what lies ahead – the goal for the prize of the upward call of God in Christ Jesus*, Phil. 3.13-14 – Brothers, I do not consider that I have made it my own. But one thing I do: forgetting what lies behind and straining forward to what lies ahead, [14] I press on toward the goal for the prize of the upward call of God in Christ Jesus.

The "Double Whammy" of Regret: Doing a Wrong and Thinking about What I Did Wrong

Part of every misery is, so to speak, the misery's shadow or reflection: the fact that you don't merely suffer but have to keep on thinking about the fact that you suffer. I not only live each endless day in grief, but live each day thinking about living each day in grief.

~ C. S. Lewis

You Can Alter the Effect of Your Memory's Past

Forgiving does not erase the bitter past. A **healed** memory is not a **deleted** memory. Instead, forgiving what we cannot forget creates a new way to remember. We change the memory of our past into a hope for our future.

~ Lewis B. Smedes

Never Underestimate the Power of Surrender

Again, the kingdom of heaven is like a merchant in search of fine pearls, who, on finding one pearl of great value, went and sold all that he had and bought it.

~ Jesus, Matthew 13.45-46

I hated every minute of training, but I said, "Don't quit. Suffer now and live the rest of your life as a champion."

~ Muhammad Ali

A hero is someone who has given his or her life to something bigger than oneself.

~ Joseph Campbell

As soldiers of Jesus Christ, called to Kingdom advance, we possess . . .

- **No Reserves:** we surrender all to Christ, without conditions
- **No Retreat:** we stand our ground for Christ, no matter what
- *No Regrets: we lose everything for what really counts, without disappointment*

Session 3 Notes

EMPOWERED TO LIVE FREE
SIAFU Men's Conference 2016

NO RESERVES RETREAT REGRETS

Stay awake, stand firm in your faith, be brave, be strong.
~ 1 Corinthians 16.13 (CEB)

APPENDIX

Appendix 1

The Story of God: Our Sacred Roots

Rev. Dr. Don L. Davis

The LORD God is the source, sustainer, and end of all things in the heavens and earth.
All things were formed and exist by his will and for his eternal glory, the triune God, Father, Son, and Holy Spirit, Rom. 11.36.

THE TRIUNE GOD'S UNFOLDING DRAMA — God's Self-Revelation in Creation, Israel, and Christ
The Objective Foundation: The Sovereign Love of God — God's Narration of His Saving Work in Christ

THE CHURCH'S PARTICIPATION IN GOD'S UNFOLDING DRAMA — Fidelity to the Apostolic Witness to Christ and His Kingdom
The Subjective Practice: Salvation by Grace through Faith — The Redeemed's Joyous Response to God's Saving Work in Christ

The Alpha and the Omega / *The Author of the Story*	Christus Victor / *The Champion of the Story*	Come, Holy Spirit / *The Interpreter of the Story*	Your Word Is Truth / *The Testimony of the Story*	The Great Confession / *The People of the Story*	His Life in Us / *Re-enactment of the Story*	Living in the Way / *Embodiment of the Story*	Reborn to Serve / *Continuation of the Story*
The Father as Director	Jesus as Lead Actor	The Spirit as Narrator	Scripture as Script	As Saints, Confessors	As Worshipers, Ministers	As Followers, Sojourners	As Servants, Ambassadors
Christian Worldview	Communal Identity	Spiritual Experience	Biblical Authority	Orthodox Theology	Priestly Worship	Congregational Discipleship	Kingdom Witness
Theistic and Trinitarian Vision	Christ-centered Foundation	Spirit-Indwelt and -Filled Community	Canonical and Apostolic Witness	Ancient Creedal Affirmation of Faith	Weekly Gathering in Christian Assembly	Corporate, Ongoing Spiritual Formation	Active Agents of the Reign of God
Sovereign Willing	Messianic Representing	Divine Comforting	Inspired Testifying	Truthful Retelling	Joyful Excelling	Faithful Indwelling	Hopeful Compelling
Creator — True Maker of the Cosmos	Recapitulation — Typos and Fulfillment of the Covenant	Life-Giver — Regeneration and Adoption	Divine Inspiration — God-breathed Word	The Confession of Faith — Union with Christ	Song and Celebration — Historical Recitation	Pastoral Oversight — Shepherding the Flock	Explicit Unity — Love for the Saints
Owner — Sovereign Disposer of Creation	Revealer — Incarnation of the Word	Teacher — Illuminator of the Truth	Sacred History — Historical Record	Baptism into Christ — Communion of Saints	Homilies and Teachings — Prophetic Proclamation	Shared Spirituality — Common Journey through the Spiritual Disciplines	Radical Hospitality — Evidence of God's Kingdom Reign
Ruler — Blessed Controller of All Things	Redeemer — Reconciler of All Things	Helper — Endowment and the Power	Biblical Theology — Divine Commentary	The Rule of Faith — Apostles' Creed and Nicene Creed	The Lord's Supper — Dramatic Re-enactment	Embodiment — Anamnesis and Prolepsis through the Church Year	Extravagant Generosity — Good Works
Covenant Keeper — Faithful Promisor	Restorer — Christ, the Victor over the powers of evil	Guide — Divine Presence and Shekinah	Spiritual Food — Sustenance for the Journey	The Vincentian Canon — Ubiquity, antiquity, universality	Eschatological Foreshadowing — The Already/Not Yet	Effective Discipling — Spiritual Formation in the Believing Assembly	Evangelical Witness — Making Disciples of All People Groups

Appendix 2

Incorporation into the People of the Story: Steps of Discipling Others into the Story of God

Rev. Dr. Don L. Davis

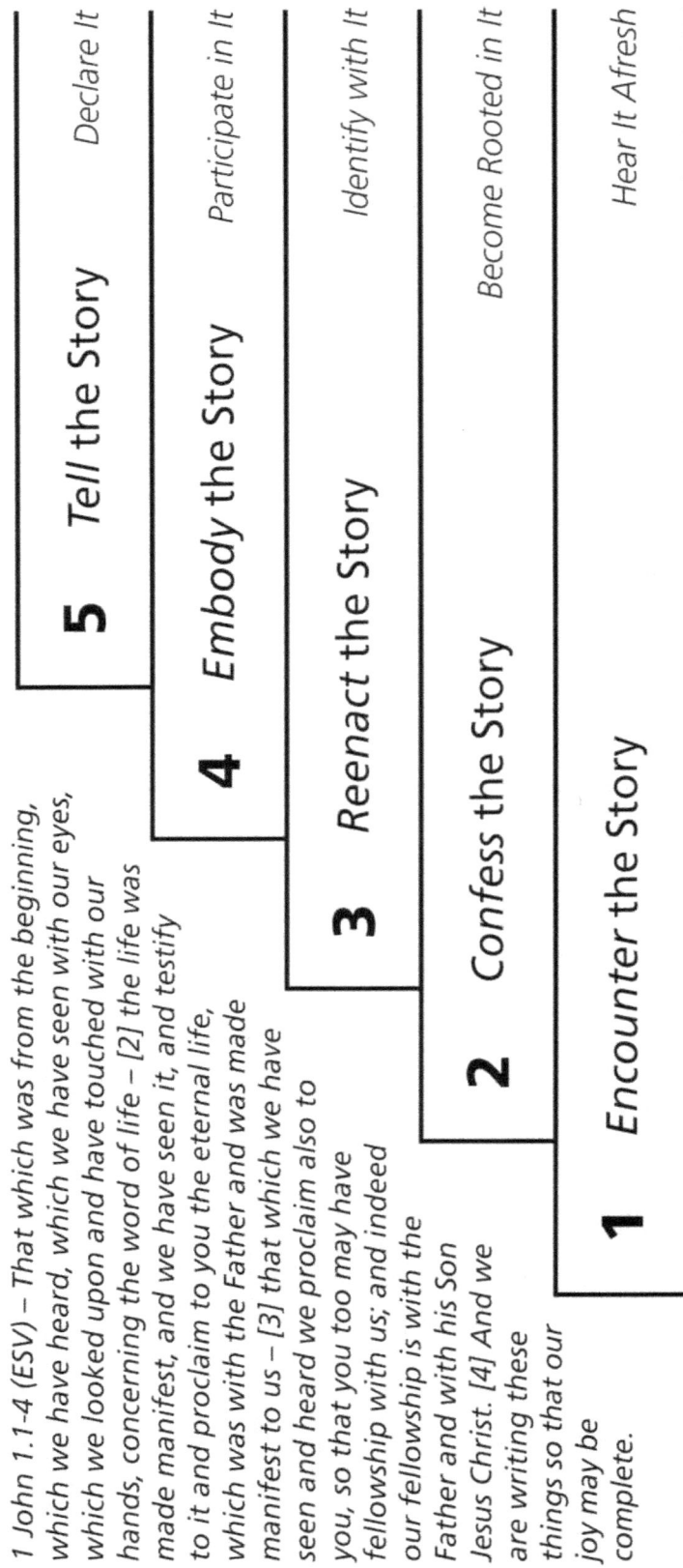

5 Tell the Story — *Declare It*

4 Embody the Story — *Participate in It*

3 Reenact the Story — *Identify with It*

2 Confess the Story — *Become Rooted in It*

1 Encounter the Story — *Hear It Afresh*

1 John 1.1-4 (ESV) – That which was from the beginning, which we have heard, which we have seen with our eyes, which we looked upon and have touched with our hands, concerning the word of life – [2] the life was made manifest, and we have seen it, and testify to it and proclaim to you the eternal life, which was with the Father and was made manifest to us – [3] that which we have seen and heard we proclaim also to you, so that you too may have fellowship with us; and indeed our fellowship is with the Father and with his Son Jesus Christ. [4] And we are writing these things so that our joy may be complete.

Luke 1.1-4 (ESV) – Inasmuch as many have undertaken to compile a narrative of the things that have been accomplished among us, [2] just as those who from the beginning were eyewitnesses and ministers of the word have delivered them to us, [3] it seemed good to me also, having followed all things closely for some time past, to write an orderly account for you, most excellent Theophilus, [4] that you may have certainty concerning the things you have been taught.

- Personal and Corporate
- Alone and Together
- Spiritual and Practical
- Devotional and Intellectual
- Historical and Contemporary

Appendix 3

The Theology of Christus Victor

Rev. Dr. Don L. Davis

	The Promised Messiah	The Word Made Flesh	The Son of Man	The Suffering Servant	The Lamb of God	The Victorious Conqueror	The Reigning Lord in Heaven	The Bridegroom and Coming King
Biblical Framework	Israel's hope of Yahweh's anointed who would redeem his people	In the person of Jesus of Nazareth, the Lord has come to the world	As the promised king and divine Son of Man, Jesus reveals the Father's glory and salvation to the world	As Inaugurator of the Kingdom of God, Jesus demonstrates God's reign present through his words, wonders, and works	As both High Priest and Paschal Lamb, Jesus offers himself to God on our behalf as a sacrifice for sin	In his resurrection from the dead and ascension to God's right hand, Jesus is proclaimed as a Victor over the power of sin and death	Now reigning at God's right hand till his enemies are made his footstool, Jesus pours out his benefits on his body	Soon the risen and ascended Lord will return to gather his Bride, the Church, and consummate his work
Scripture References	Isa. 9.6-7 Jer. 23.5-6 Isa. 11.1-10	John 1.14-18 Matt. 1.20-23 Phil. 2.6-8	Matt. 2.1-11 Num. 24.17 Luke 1.78-79	Mark 1.14-15 Matt. 12.25-30 Luke 17.20-21	2 Cor. 5.18-21 Isa. 52-53 John 1.29	Eph. 1.16-23 Phil. 2.5-11 Col. 1.15-20	1 Cor. 15.25 Eph. 4.15-16 Acts. 2.32-36	Rom. 14.7-9 Rev. 5.9-13 1 Thess. 4.13-18
Jesus' History	The pre-incarnate, only begotten Son of God in glory	His conception by the Spirit, and birth to Mary	His manifestation to the Magi and to the world	His teaching, exorcisms, miracles, and mighty works among the people	His suffering, crucifixion, death, and burial	His resurrection, with appearances to his witnesses, and his ascension to the Father	The sending of the Holy Spirit and his gifts, and Christ's session in heaven at the Father's right hand	His soon return from heaven to earth as Lord and Christ: the Second Coming
Description	The biblical promise for the seed of Abraham, the prophet like Moses, the son of David	In the Incarnation, God has come to us; Jesus reveals to humankind the Father's glory in fullness	In Jesus, God has shown his salvation to the entire world, including the Gentiles	In Jesus, the promised Kingdom of God has come visibly to earth, demonstrating his binding of Satan and rescinding the Curse	As God's perfect Lamb, Jesus offers himself up to God as a sin offering on behalf of the entire world	In his resurrection and ascension, Jesus destroyed death, disarmed Satan, and rescinded the Curse	Jesus is installed at the Father's right hand as Head of the Church, Firstborn from the dead, and supreme Lord in heaven	As we labor in his harvest field in the world, so we await Christ's return, the fulfillment of his promise
Church Year	Advent	Christmas	Season after Epiphany Baptism and Transfiguration	Lent	Holy Week Passion	Eastertide Easter, Ascension Day, Pentecost	Season after Pentecost Trinity Sunday	Season after Pentecost All Saints Day, Reign of Christ the King
Spiritual Formation	*The Coming of Christ* As we await his Coming, let us proclaim and affirm the hope of Christ	*The Birth of Christ* O Word made flesh, let us every heart prepare him room to dwell	*The Manifestation of Christ* Divine Son of Man, show the nations your salvation and glory	*The Ministry of Christ* In the person of Christ, the power of the reign of God has come to earth and to the Church	*The Suffering and Death of Christ* May those who share the Lord's death be resurrected with him	*The Resurrection and Ascension of Christ* Let us participate by faith in the victory of Christ over the power of sin, Satan, and death	*The Heavenly Session of Christ* Come, indwell us, Holy Spirit, and empower us to advance Christ's Kingdom in the world	*The Reign of Christ* We live and work in expectation of his soon return, seeking to please him in all things

Appendix 4

Christus Victor: An Integrated Vision for the Christian Life and Witness

Rev. Dr. Don L. Davis

For the Church

- The Church is the primary extension of Jesus in the world
- Ransomed treasure of the victorious, risen Christ
- *Laos:* The people of God
- God's new creation: presence of the future
- Locus and agent of the Already/Not Yet Kingdom

For Gifts

- God's gracious endowments and benefits from *Christus Victor*
- Pastoral offices to the Church
- The Holy Spirit's sovereign dispensing of the gifts
- Stewardship: divine, diverse gifts for the common good

For Theology and Doctrine

- The authoritative Word of Christ's victory: the Apostolic Tradition: the Holy Scriptures
- Theology as commentary on the grand narrative of God
- *Christus Victor* as core theological framework for meaning in the world
- The Nicene Creed: the Story of God's triumphant grace

For Evangelism and Mission

- Evangelism as unashamed declaration and demonstration of *Christus Victor* to the world
- The Gospel as Good News of kingdom pledge
- We proclaim God's Kingdom come in the person of Jesus of Nazareth
- The Great Commission: go to all people groups making disciples of Christ and his Kingdom
- Proclaiming Christ as Lord and Messiah

Christus Victor

Destroyer of Evil and Death
Restorer of Creation
Victor o'er Hades and Sin
Crusher of Satan

For Spirituality

- The Holy Spirit's presence and power in the midst of God's people
- Sharing in the disciplines of the Spirit
- Gatherings, lectionary, liturgy, and our observances in the Church Year
- Living the life of the risen Christ in the rhythm of our ordinary lives

For Worship

- People of the Resurrection: unending celebration of the people of God
- Remembering, participating in the Christ event in our worship
- Listen and respond to the Word
- Transformed at the Table, the Lord's Supper
- The presence of the Father through the Son in the Spirit

For Justice and Compassion

- The gracious and generous expressions of Jesus through the Church
- The Church displays the very life of the Kingdom
- The Church demonstrates the very life of the Kingdom of heaven right here and now
- Having freely received, we freely give (no sense of merit or pride)
- Justice as tangible evidence of the Kingdom come

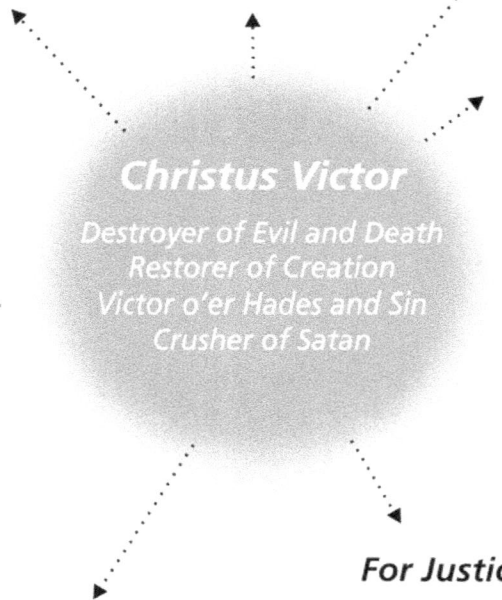

Appendix 5

Ladd's View of Time

Rev. Dr. Don L. Davis

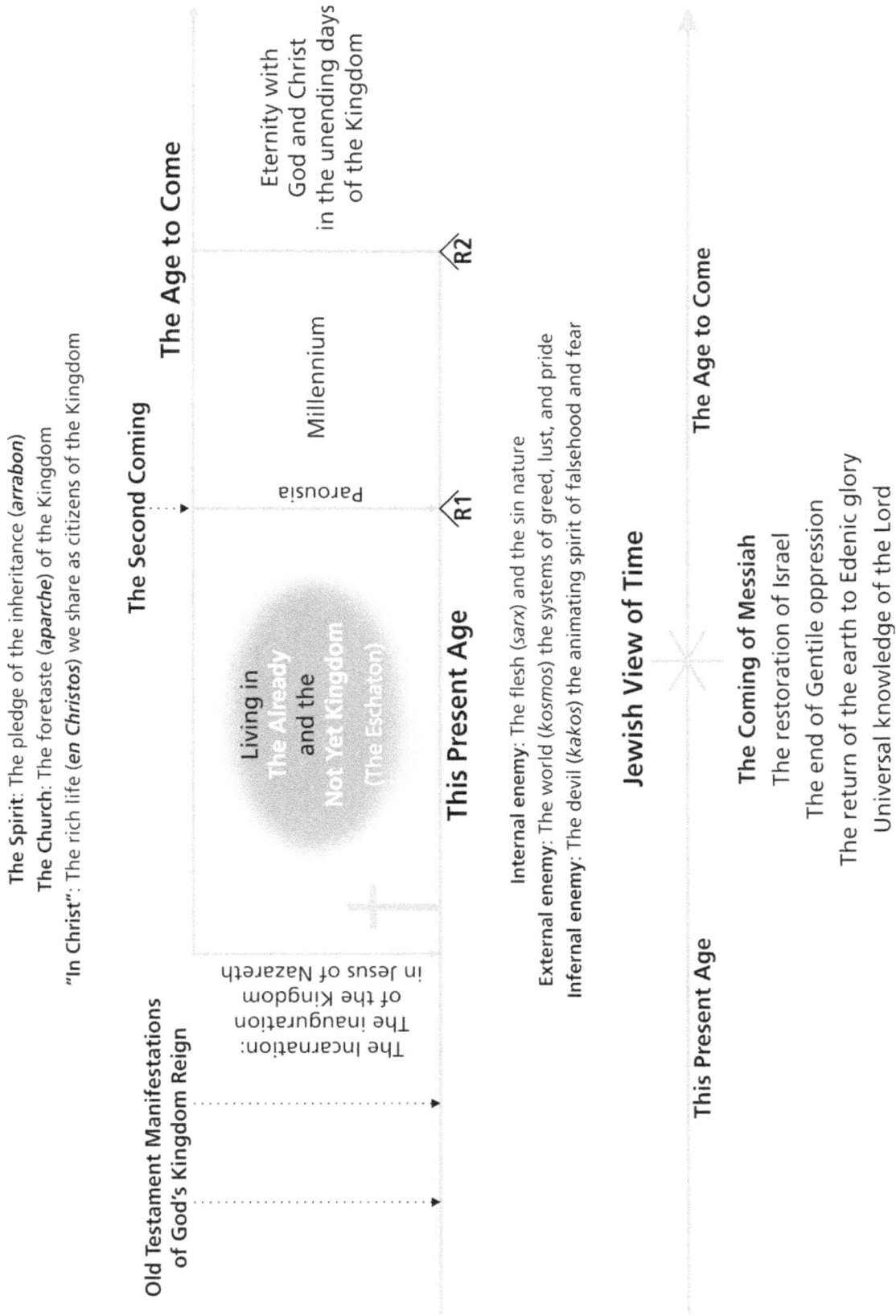

Ladd's View of Time

The Spirit: The pledge of the inheritance (*arrabon*)

The Church: The foretaste (*aparche*) of the Kingdom

"In Christ": The rich life (*en Christos*) we share as citizens of the Kingdom

The Second Coming

The Age to Come

Eternity with God and Christ in the unending days of the Kingdom

Parousia

Millennium

R2

R1

Living in
The Already
and the
Not Yet Kingdom
(The Eschaton)

This Present Age

Old Testament Manifestations of God's Kingdom Reign

The Incarnation:
The inauguration of the Kingdom in Jesus of Nazareth

Internal enemy: The flesh (*sarx*) and the sin nature

External enemy: The world (*kosmos*) the systems of greed, lust, and pride

Infernal enemy: The devil (*kakos*) the animating spirit of falsehood and fear

Jewish View of Time

The Age to Come

The Coming of Messiah

The restoration of Israel

The end of Gentile oppression

The return of the earth to Edenic glory

Universal knowledge of the Lord

This Present Age

Appendix 6

Jesus of Nazareth: The Presence of the Future

Rev. Dr. Don L. Davis

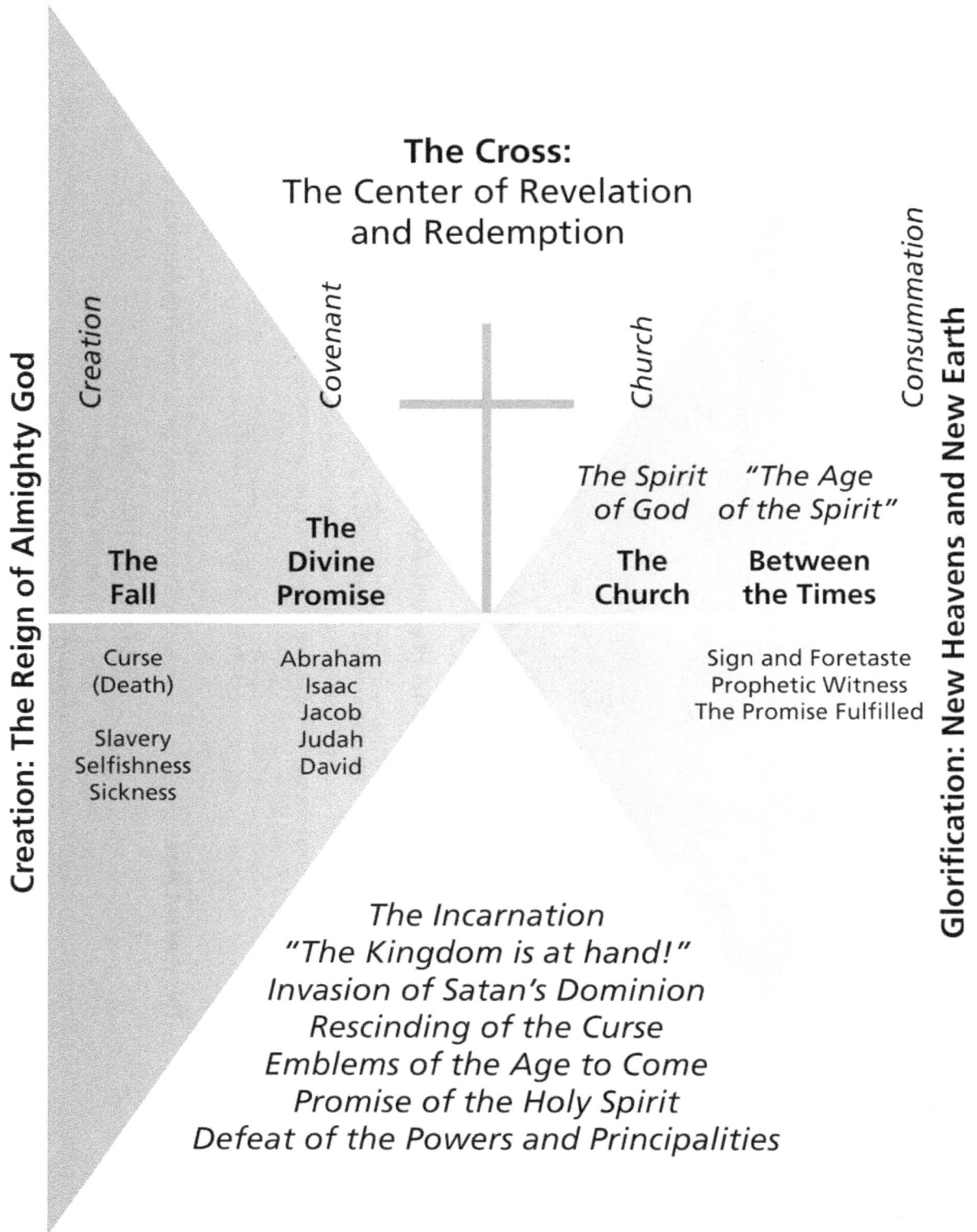

The Cross:
The Center of Revelation
and Redemption

Creation

Covenant

Church

Consummation

Creation: The Reign of Almighty God

Glorification: New Heavens and New Earth

The Spirit *"The Age*
of God *of the Spirit"*

The
Fall

The
Divine
Promise

The
Church

Between
the Times

Curse
(Death)

Slavery
Selfishness
Sickness

Abraham
Isaac
Jacob
Judah
David

Sign and Foretaste
Prophetic Witness
The Promise Fulfilled

The Incarnation
"The Kingdom is at hand!"
Invasion of Satan's Dominion
Rescinding of the Curse
Emblems of the Age to Come
Promise of the Holy Spirit
Defeat of the Powers and Principalities

Appendix 7
The Cost of Discipleship
Rev. Dr. Don L. Davis

"You can pay me now, or you can pay me later."

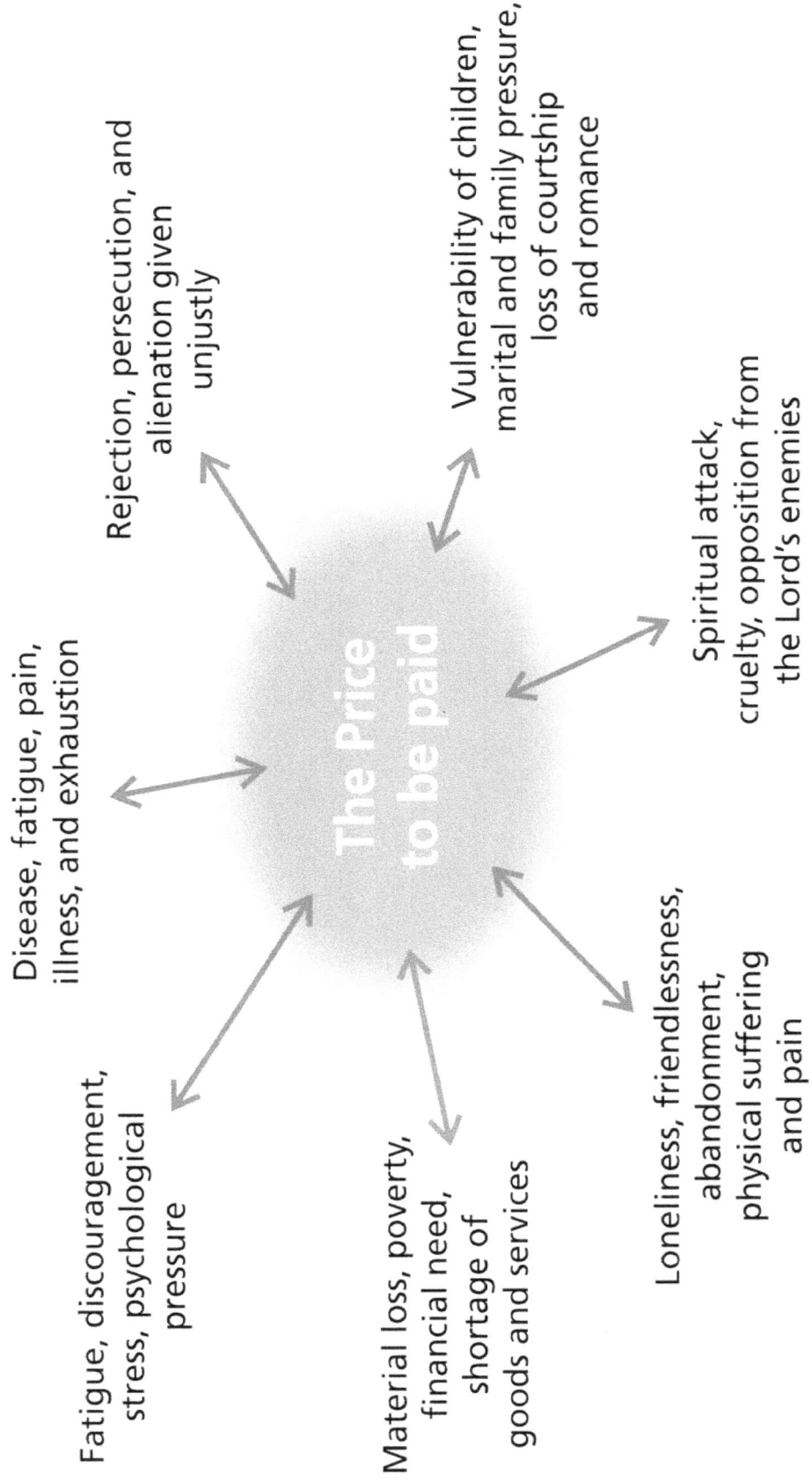

The Price to be paid

Rejection, persecution, and alienation given unjustly

Vulnerability of children, marital and family pressure, loss of courtship and romance

Disease, fatigue, pain, illness, and exhaustion

Spiritual attack, cruelty, opposition from the Lord's enemies

Fatigue, discouragement, stress, psychological pressure

Material loss, poverty, financial need, shortage of goods and services

Loneliness, friendlessness, abandonment, physical suffering and pain

Appendix 8

Substitue Centers to a Christ-Centered Vision

Goods and Effects Which Our Culture Substitutes as the Ultimate Concern

Rev. Dr. Don L. Davis

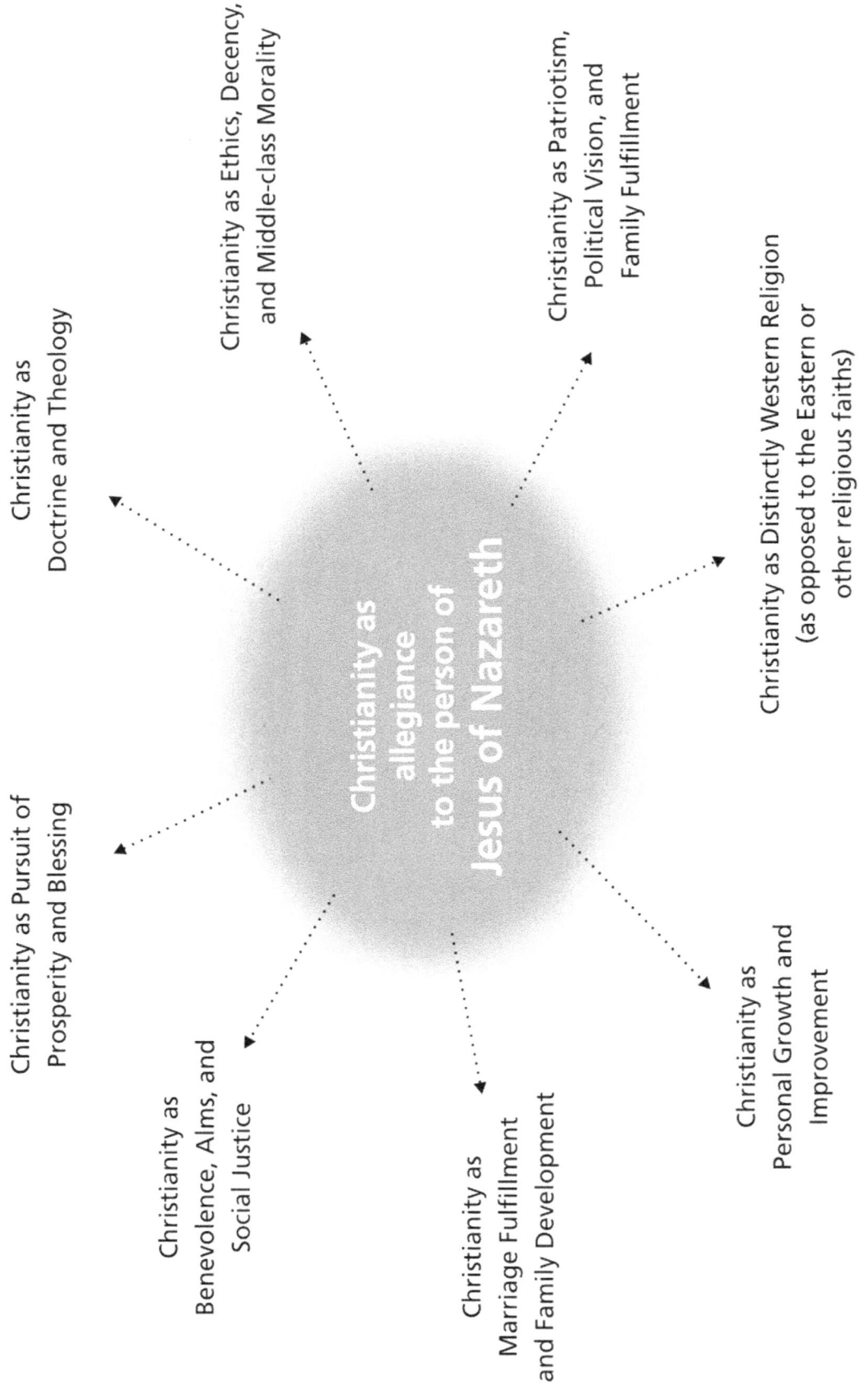

Christianity as
Doctrine and Theology

Christianity as Ethics, Decency,
and Middle-class Morality

Christianity as Patriotism,
Political Vision, and
Family Fulfillment

Christianity as
Pursuit of
Prosperity and Blessing

**Christianity as
allegiance
to the person of
Jesus of Nazareth**

Christianity as Distinctly Western Religion
(as opposed to the Eastern or
other religious faiths)

Christianity as
Benevolence, Alms, and
Social Justice

Christianity as
Marriage Fulfillment
and Family Development

Christianity as
Personal Growth and
Improvement

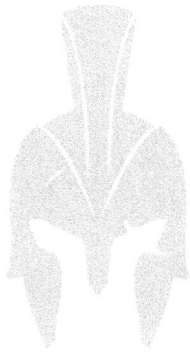

Appendix 9
The Importance of Discipline
Rev. Dr. Don L. Davis

Discipline is what moderns need the most and want the least.

Too often young people who leave home, students who quit school, husbands and wives who seek divorce, church members who neglect services, employees who walk out on their jobs are simply trying to escape discipline. The true motive may often be camouflaged by a hundred excuses, but behind the flimsy front is the hard core of aversion to restraint and control.

Much of our restlessness and instability can be traced to this basic fault in modern character. Our overflowing asylums and hospitals and jails are but symptoms of an undisciplined age. There may be many secondary causes and there may be many secondary cures, but somewhere behind them all is the need for discipline. The kind of discipline needed is far deeper than the rule of alarm clocks and time cards; it embraces self-restraint, courage, perseverance, and resiliency as the inner panoply of the soul.

Many nervous and emotional disorders are the accumulated result of years of self-indulgent living. I am not thinking of the drunkards or the libertines, but of the respectable Christians who probably would be horrified at the thought of touching liquor or indulging in gross immorality. But they are nevertheless undisciplined, and the fatal weakness is unmasked in the day of trial and adversity. A lifelong pattern of running away from difficulties, of avoiding incompatible people, of seeking the easy way, of quitting when the going gets rough finally shows up in a neurotic semi-invalidism and incapactiy. Numerous books may be read, many doctors and preachers consulted, innumerable prayers may be offered, and religious commitments made; the patient may be inundated with drugs, advice, costly treatment, and spiritual scourgings; yet none lay bare the real cause: lack of discipline. And the only real cure is to become a disciplined person.

~ Richard Shelly Taylor. *The Disciplined Life*.
Kansas City: Beacon Hill Press, 1962. pp. 10-11

Key questions for understanding the role of discipline in God's call to holiness

1. Is discipline the same as holiness?

2. Are there any cases where discipline can become a substitute for holiness?

3. Can discipline bring about or produce holiness?

4. If discipline does not produce holiness, then what are the benefits of discipline for us?

5. For growing Christians and ministers, what is the most biblical way to understand the relationship of discipline to holiness?

Appendix 10

Understanding Leadership as Representation: The Six Stages of Formal Proxy

Rev. Dr. Don L. Davis

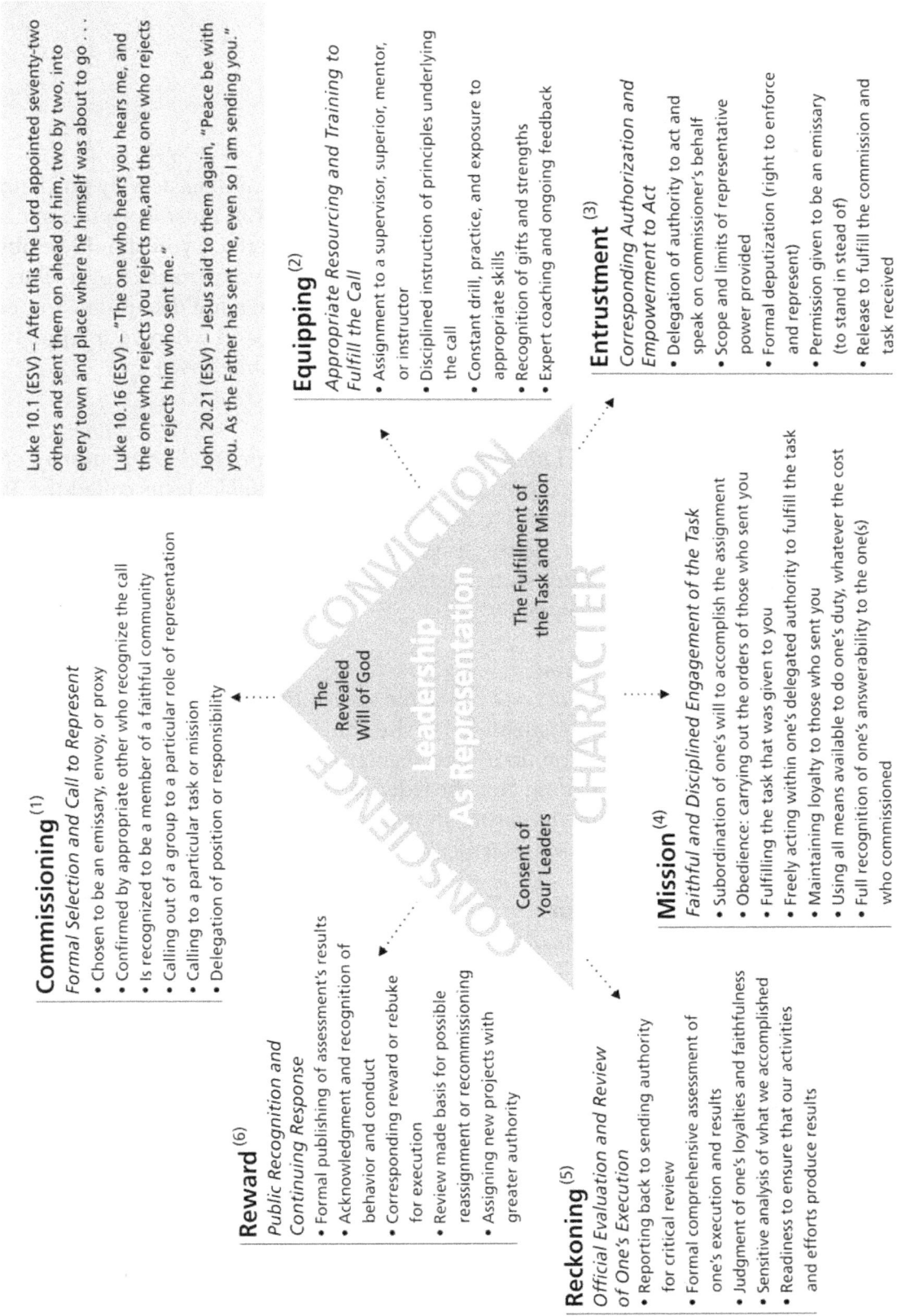

Commissioning [1]
Formal Selection and Call to Represent
- Chosen to be an emissary, envoy, or proxy
- Confirmed by appropriate other who recognize the call
- Is recognized to be a member of a faithful community
- Calling out of a group to a particular role of representation
- Calling to a particular task or mission
- Delegation of position or responsibility

Luke 10.1 (ESV) – After this the Lord appointed seventy-two others and sent them on ahead of him, two by two, into every town and place where he himself was about to go . . .

Luke 10.16 (ESV) – "The one who hears you hears me, and the one who rejects you rejects me, and the one who rejects me rejects him who sent me."

John 20.21 (ESV) – Jesus said to them again, "Peace be with you. As the Father has sent me, even so I am sending you."

Equipping [2]
Appropriate Resourcing and Training to Fulfill the Call
- Assignment to a supervisor, superior, mentor, or instructor
- Disciplined instruction of principles underlying the call
- Constant drill, practice, and exposure to appropriate skills
- Recognition of gifts and strengths
- Expert coaching and ongoing feedback

Entrustment [3]
Corresponding Authorization and Empowerment to Act
- Delegation of authority to act and speak on commissioner's behalf
- Scope and limits of representative power provided
- Formal deputization (right to enforce and represent)
- Permission given to be an emissary (to stand in stead of)
- Release to fulfill the commission and task received

CONVICTION
CONSCIENCE
CHARACTER

The Revealed Will of God

Leadership As Representation

The Fulfillment of the Task and Mission

Consent of Your Leaders

Mission [4]
Faithful and Disciplined Engagement of the Task
- Subordination of one's will to accomplish the assignment
- Obedience: carrying out the orders of those who sent you
- Fulfilling the task that was given to you
- Freely acting within one's delegated authority to fulfill the task
- Maintaining loyalty to those who sent you
- Using all means available to do one's duty, whatever the cost
- Full recognition of one's answerability to the one(s) who commissioned

Reckoning [5]
Official Evaluation and Review of One's Execution
- Reporting back to sending authority for critical review
- Formal comprehensive assessment of one's execution and results
- Judgment of one's loyalties and faithfulness
- Sensitive analysis of what we accomplished
- Readiness to ensure that our activities and efforts produce results

Reward [6]
Public Recognition and Continuing Response
- Formal publishing of assessment's results
- Acknowledgment and recognition of behavior and conduct
- Corresponding reward or rebuke for execution
- Review made basis for possible reassignment or recommissioning
- Assigning new projects with greater authority

Appendix 11
Steps to Equipping Others
Rev. Dr. Don L. Davis

Step One

You become a Master at it, striving toward mastery by practicing it with regularity, excellence, and enjoyment. You must learn to do it, and do it excellently. While you need not be perfect, you should be able to do it, be doing it regularly, and growing in your practice of it. This is the most fundamental principle of all mentoring and discipling. You cannot teach what you do not know or cannot do, and when your Apprentice is fully trained, they will become like you (Luke 6.40).

Step Two

You select an Apprentice who also desires to develop mastery of the thing, one who is teachable, faithful, and available. Jesus called the Twelve to be with him, and to send them out to preach (Mark 3.14). His relationship was clear, neither vague nor coerced. The roles and responsibilities of the relationship must be carefully outlined, clearly discussed, and openly agreed upon.

Step Three

You instruct and model the task in the presence of and accompanied by your Apprentice. He/she comes alongside you to listen, observe, and watch. You do it with regularity and excellence, and your Apprentice comes along "for the ride," who is brought along to see how it is done. A picture is worth a thousand words. This sort of non-pressure participant observation is critical to in-depth training (2 Tim. 2.2; Phil. 4.9).

Step Four

You do the task and practice the thing together. Having modeled the act for your Apprentice in many ways and at many times, you now invite them to cooperate with you by becoming a partner-in-training, working together on the task. The goal is to do the task together, taking mutual responsibility. You coordinate your efforts, working together in harmony to accomplish the thing.

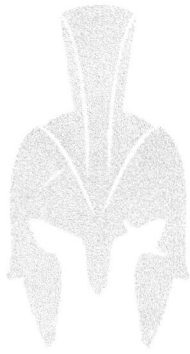

Step Five

*Your Apprentice does the task on their own, **in the presence of and accompanied by you**.* You provide opportunity to your Apprentice to practice the thing in your presence while you watch and listen. You make yourself available to help, but offer it in the background; you provide counsel, input, and guidance as they request it, but they do the task. Afterwards, you evaluate and clarify anything you may have observed as you accompanied your Apprentice (2 Cor. 11.1).

Step Six

*Your Apprentice does the thing solo, practicing it regularly, automatically, and excellently **until mastery of the thing is gained**.* After your Apprentice has done the task under your supervision excellently, he/she is ready to be released to make the thing his/her own by habituating the act in his/her own life. You are a co-doer with your Apprentice; both of you are doing the task without coercion or aid from the other. The goal is familiarity and skillfulness in the task (Heb. 5.11-15).

Step Seven

*Your Apprentice **becomes a Mentor of others**, selecting other faithful Apprentices to equip and train.* The training process bears fruit when the Apprentice, having mastered the thing you have equipped him/her to do, becomes a trainer of others. This is the heart of the discipling and training process (Heb. 5.11-14; 2 Tim. 2.2).

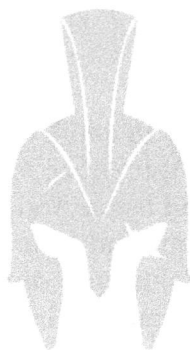

Appendix 12

An Outline for a Vision for Discipleship

"Let's Give Jesus Christ Our Best and All"

Rev. Dr. Don L. Davis

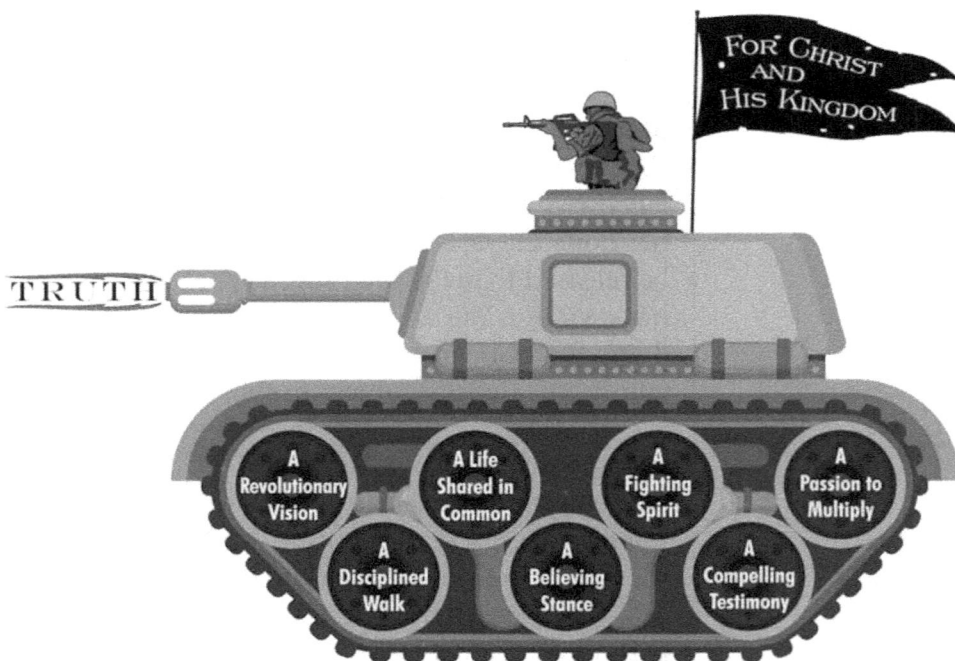

I. A Zeal to Represent – Represents Jesus and the Kingdom in everything – **LET'S**

   A. **L** - *Lives* above all else as an ambassador of Jesus Christ and his Kingdom
       2 Cor. 5.18-21; John 20.21; Acts 26.16-18; Mal. 2.7

   B. **E** - *Eager* to declare and display Jesus as Lord of all everywhere in everything
       2 Cor. 4.3-5; Acts 2.36; 5.31; Rom. 14.7-9; 1 Cor. 8.5-6; Phil. 2.8-11

   C. **T** - *Takes* seriously responsibility to defend Jesus' reputation
       Phil. 2.21; Gal. 1.10; James 4.4; 2 Cor. 5.9-11; Acts 4.19; 5.29

   D. **S** - *Strives* to represent kingdom values in all affairs, no matter what the cost
       2 Tim. 2.3-10; Acts 20.22-24; 2 Tim. 3.15

II. A Revolutionary Vision – Interprets everything through the Story and the Mind of Christ – **GIVE**

    A. **G** - *Gives* his whole heart to take on Christ's yoke, and to learn and become like him,
Matt. 11.28-30; John 14.21-24; Acts 3.22-23; Luke 10.39-42; 1 John 2.6

    B. **I** - *Identifies* with God's people in the Story of the Scriptures,
1 Cor. 10.1-11; Heb. 11.32-40

    C. **V** - *Views* everything as it relates to God, his purposes, and his people
2 Cor. 10.3-5; Isa. 55.8-11; 1 Cor. 2.9-16; Eph. 4.20-24

    D. **E** - *Eats*, drinks, and sleeps the story of God in Christ (master the Bible Story)
2 Tim. 3.15-17; John 8.31-32; Matt. 4.4, cf. Deut. 8.1-3; Matt. 28.19-20

III. A Disciplined Walk – Practices fervently and regularly the personal and corporate disciplines – **JESUS**

    A. **J** - *Jesus* is crowned Lord in living sacrifice every day
Rom. 12.1-2; Phil. 2.5-11; Luke 9.23; Rom. 6.1-11; Col. 3.1-4

    B. **E** - *Experiences* God's presence daily in the fellowship of the Word and prayer
Isa. 50.4; 57.15-19; 1 John 5.5-10; Exod. 4.11-12; John 10.1-6; Ps. 5.1-3

    C. **S** - *Spirit's* filling is actively sought, his leadings are promptly obeyed
John 14.16-18; Eph. 5.18; Rom. 5.5; 14.17; 15.13; Gal. 5.15-23; Acts 9.31; 1 Thess. 5.19-21

    D. **U** - *Uses* personal discipline of body, mind, and soul to sustain spiritual vitality
1 Tim. 4.7-9; 1 Cor. 9.24-27; 2 Cor. 6.4; 11.27; Col. 3.5; 2 Tim. 2.22; 1 Pet. 2.11

    E. **S** - *Spiritual* disciplines are practiced with other followers of Jesus faithfully
Heb. 3.12-13; 10.24-25; John 13.34-35

IV. A Life Shared in Common – Fleshes out Jesus' love in marriage, family, church, and friendships – **CHRIST**

A. **C** - *Cares* for his wife as Christ loves the Church
Eph. 5.22-33; 1 Pet. 3.7; Col. 3.19

B. **H** - *Honors* father and mother, and kin in the Lord
Eph. 6.1-3; Prov. 1.8; 6.21; 23.22; 30.11,17; 1 Tim. 5.8,16

C. **R** - *Raises* children in the Lord's nurture and admonition
Gen. 18.19; Ps. 71.17-18; Prov. 19.18; 22.6,15; 29.17; Eph. 6.4; Col. 3.21; Heb. 12.7-10

D. **I** - *Identifies* as proud member of the people of God within a local church
Rom. 12.3-8; 1 Cor. 12.12-27; 1 Pet. 4.10-11; 1 Pet. 2.8-9

E. **S** - *Stands* up for his brothers and friends with unfailing loyalty: SIAFU
John 13.34-35; 1 John 3.14-16; 4.7-8; John 13.13-17; Matt. 20.25-28; 2 Tim. 2.2; 1 Cor.13.1-8

F. **T** - *Takes* every opportunity to give to, build up, and bless generously God's people
Gal. 5.1-13; 1 Pet. 2.4-5; Rom. 15.1-2; 1 Cor. 8.10-13

V. A Believing Stance – Learns, masters, and defends the apostolic faith – **OUR**

A. **O** - *Operates* by the Word of the Lord , not on how things look, feel, or what others think
Ps. 1; John 8.31-32; 2 Pet. 1.20-21; 1 Pet. 1.22-25; James 1.22-25; 2 Tim. 3.16-17; Heb. 11.6; Rom. 10.17; 2 Cor. 5.7; 2 Tim. 2.15; 2 Cor. 10.3-5; 4.17-18; John 8.44

B. **U** - *Unwilling* to stand for or speak anything that compromises God's truth
2 Cor. 4.13-18; Prov. 18.21; Rom. 3.3-4; 2 John 8-11; Gal. 1.7-10; Col. 2.6-10; 2 Cor. 5.18-21; John 20.21

C. **R** - *Ready* and willing to defend the apostolic faith (the Nicene Creed)
1 Cor. 15.1-8; 2 Tim. 2.15; Jude 3-4; 1 John 1.1-4; 2 Cor. 10.3-6; 1 Pet. 3.14-16

VI. A Fighting Spirit – Fights the good fight as a soldier of Jesus Christ – **BEST**

    A. **B** - *Boldness* to fight God's enemies (i.e., world, flesh, and the devil) in Christ's strength
       1 John 2.15-17; Gal. 5.15-23; 1 Pet. 2.11; Rom. 7.14-25; John 8.44; 1 Pet. 5.7-8; Eph. 6.10-18; 2 Cor. 10.3-5; 11.13-15

    B. **E** - *Exercises* faith that overcomes in daily spiritual warfare
       Heb. 11.6; Rom. 1.17; 2 Chron. 20.20; Ps. 62.8; Isa. 7.9; Mark 9.23; 11.22-24; Rom. 4.18-25; 1 John 5.4; 4.4; Rev. 12.11; Rom. 8.35-39

    C. **S** - *Shrinks* back from no challenge or opportunity God provides, however difficult
       2 Cor. 11.22-33; 2 Tim. 3.12; Acts 14.21-22; Heb. 12.1-3; 1 Pet. 2.21-25; Gal. 6.7-9

    D. **T** - *Takes* seriously the need for self-control in all areas (e.g., of the tongue, purity, money, and attitude)
       Gal. 5.22-23; 1 Thess. 4.1-7; 1 Cor. 6.15-20; Eph. 4.25-32; 1 Cor. 6.9-12; 2 Cor. 7.1; Col. 3.5-11

VII. A Compelling Testimony – Maintains godly reputation in all public and private affairs – **AND**

    A. **A** - *Acknowledged* to be a man of excellence and principle (i.e., a man of conscience and conviction that does not yield to impulses or intimidation)
       Prov. 20.6; Dan. 3.18; 6.10; Ps. 15.1-5; Matt. 7.24-27; Acts 4.19-20; 5.29; Gal. 1.10

    B. **N** - *Neighbor* love is shown on behalf of the vulnerable (e.g., strangers, prisoners, the weak, and poor)
       Luke 4.18; James 1.29; 2 Cor. 8.9; James 2.14-16; Matt. 25.31-46; Isa. 58.5-12; Prov. 24.11-12; 1 John 3.16-18

    C. **D** - *Demonstrates* moderation and integrity in all things before outsiders (i.e., work, neighborhood, associations, etc.).
       Ps. 90.2; Matt. 5.39-42; Luke 6.29-35; Phil. 4.5; 1 Cor. 6.7; 7.29-31; Titus 3.2; Heb. 13.5-6; Matt. 10.16; Eph. 5.15-17; Col. 4.5; 1 Cor. 5.12-13; 1 Thess. 4.12; 1 Tim. 3.7; 1 Pet. 3.14-17

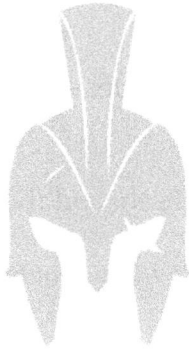

VIII. A Passion to Multiply – Offers all he is and has to multiply disciples in significant numbers among those who do not know Jesus – **ALL**

A. **A** - *Aggressively* shares his testimony with those in his *oikos* to win the lost to Christ
Ps. 119.46; 1 Pet. 3.15; Dan. 3.16-18; Amos 7.14-17; Rom. 1.15-17; Luke 21.14-15; Col. 4.6; 2 Tim. 2.24-26; John 1.40-51; Acts 10.24-33; 16.30-34; Rom. 9.1-3

B. **L** - *Lays* aside personal weekly time and effort to disciple other brothers in the Lord
Matt. 28.19-20; 2 Tim. 2.2; John 21.15-17; Acts 14.22-23; 20.28; Rom. 15.14; Eph. 4.11-15; 1 Thess. 2.5-12; Phil. 1.25-26

C. **L** - *Links* up with other brothers and churches to support missions locally and around the world (wherever Jesus is not known)
Acts 1.8; Mark 16.15; Gal. 2.6-10; Rom. 15.15-21; 1 Cor. 9.18-23; Acts 20.18-35

Appendix 13
Living as an Oikos Ambassador
Rev. Dr. Don L. Davis

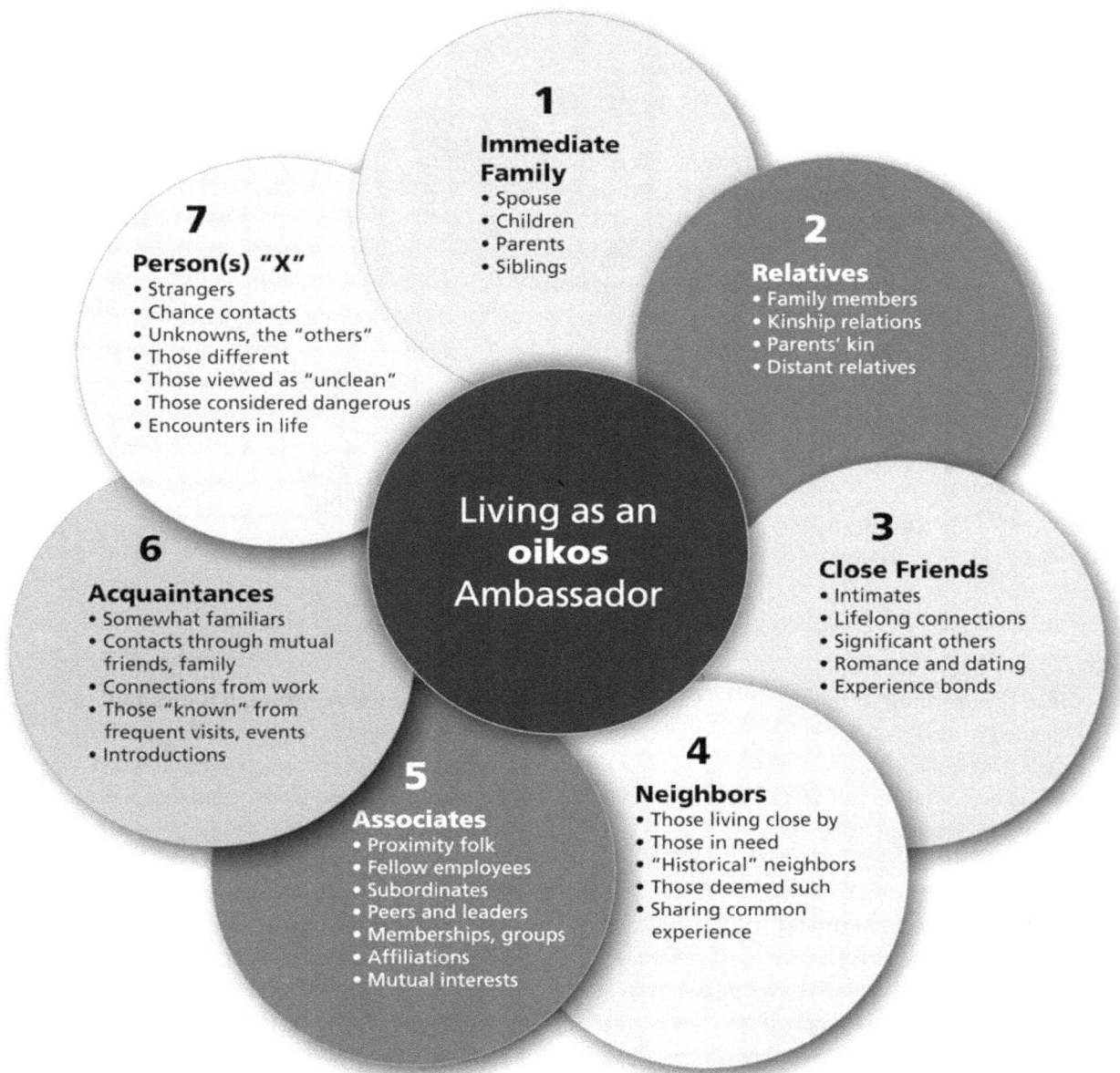

1
Immediate Family
- Spouse
- Children
- Parents
- Siblings

2
Relatives
- Family members
- Kinship relations
- Parents' kin
- Distant relatives

3
Close Friends
- Intimates
- Lifelong connections
- Significant others
- Romance and dating
- Experience bonds

4
Neighbors
- Those living close by
- Those in need
- "Historical" neighbors
- Those deemed such
- Sharing common experience

5
Associates
- Proximity folk
- Fellow employees
- Subordinates
- Peers and leaders
- Memberships, groups
- Affiliations
- Mutual interests

6
Acquaintances
- Somewhat familiars
- Contacts through mutual friends, family
- Connections from work
- Those "known" from frequent visits, events
- Introductions

7
Person(s) "X"
- Strangers
- Chance contacts
- Unknowns, the "others"
- Those different
- Those viewed as "unclean"
- Those considered dangerous
- Encounters in life

Living as an **oikos** Ambassador

Appendix 14

The Oikos Factor: Spheres of Relationship and Influence

Rev. Dr. Don L. Davis

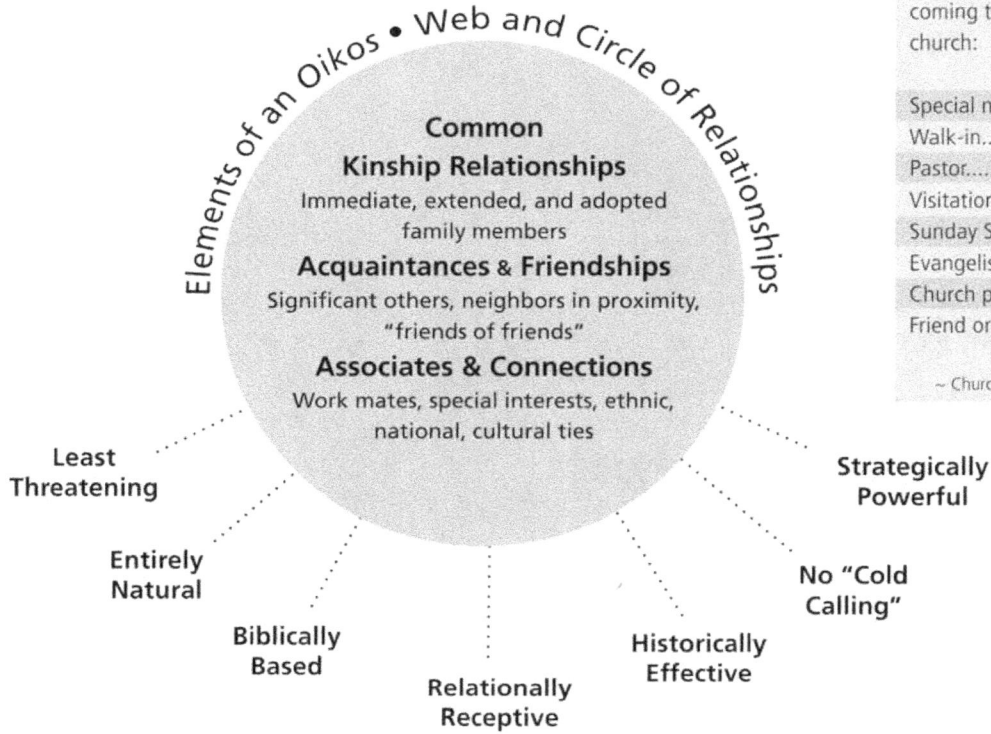

Survey: 42,000 asked: Who or what was responsible for your coming to Christ and your church:

Special need......................1-2%
Walk-in.............................2-3%
Pastor.............................5-6%
Visitation.........................1-2%
Sunday School..................4-5%
Evangelistic crusade/TV.....1/2%
Church program...............2-3%
Friend or relative.......75-90%!!

~ Church Growth, Inc. Monrovia, CA

Elements of an Oikos • Web and Circle of Relationships

**Common
Kinship Relationships**
Immediate, extended, and adopted
family members
Acquaintances & Friendships
Significant others, neighbors in proximity,
"friends of friends"
Associates & Connections
Work mates, special interests, ethnic,
national, cultural ties

Least
Threatening

Strategically
Powerful

Entirely
Natural

No "Cold
Calling"

Biblically
Based

Historically
Effective

Relationally
Receptive

Oikos (household) in the OT

"A household usually contained four generations, including men, married women, unmarried daughters, slaves of both sexes, persons without citizenship, and 'sojourners,' or resident foreign workers."

— *Hans Walter Wolff, Anthology of the Old Testament.*

Oikos (household) in the NT

Evangelism and disciple making in our NT narratives are often described as following the flow of the relational networks of various people within their *oikoi* (households), that is, those natural lines of connection in which they resided and lived (c.f., Mark 5.19; Luke 19.9; John 4.53; 1.41-45, etc.). Andrew to Simon (John 1.41-45), and both Cornelius (Acts 10-11) and the Philippian jailer (Acts 16) are notable cases of evangelism and discipling through *oikoi*.

Oikos (household) among the urban poor

While great differences exist between cultures, kinship relationships, special interest groups, and family structures among urban populations, it is clear that urbanites connect with others far more on the basis of connections through relationships, friendships, and family than through proximity and neighborhood alone. Often times the closest friends of urban poor dwellers are not immediately close by in terms of neighborhood; family and friends may dwell blocks, even miles away. Taking the time to study the precise linkages of relationships among the dwellers in a certain area can prove extremely helpful in determining the most effective strategies for evangelism and disciple making in inner city contexts.

Appendix 15

Elements of an Oikos

Rev. Dr. Don L. Davis

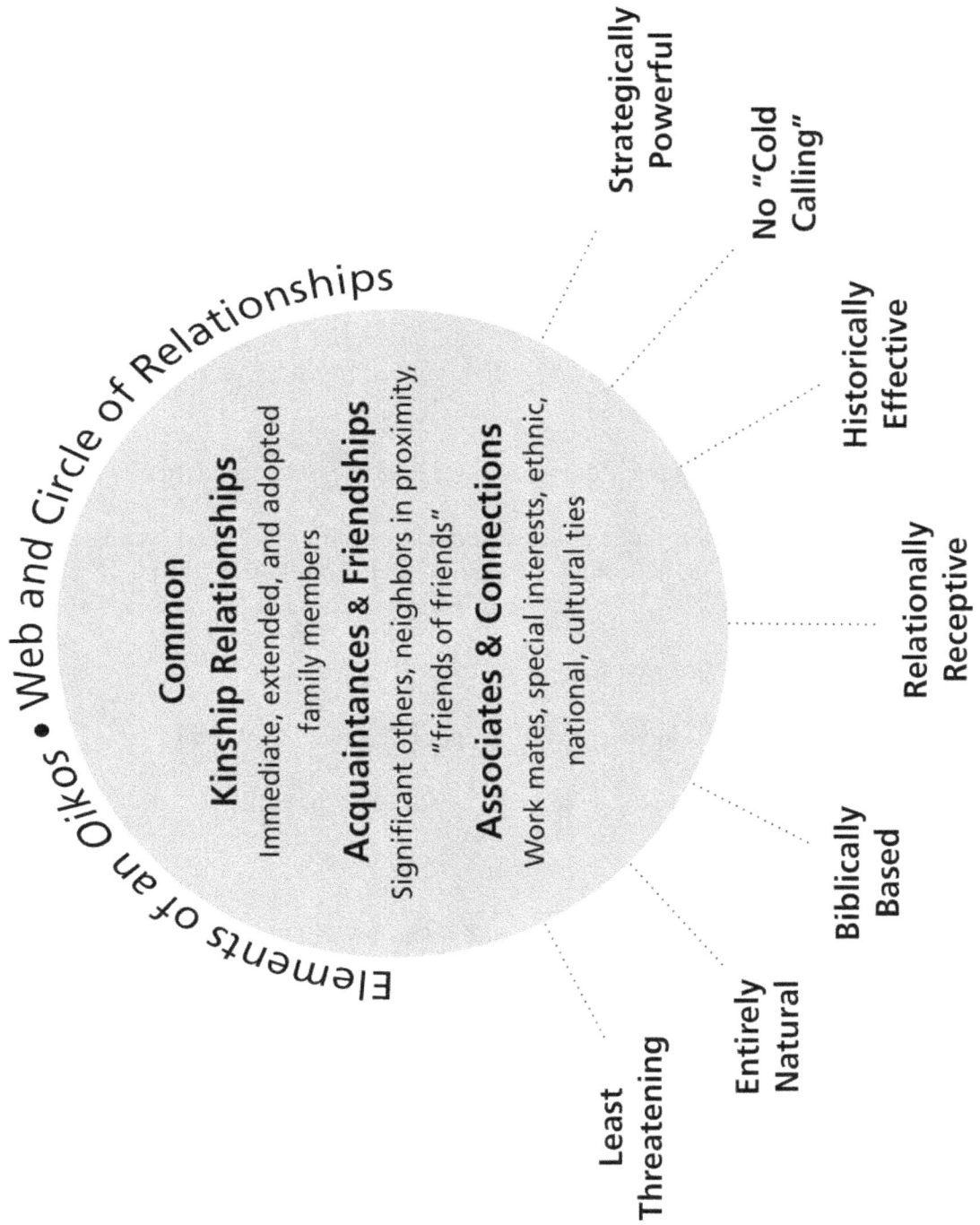

Elements of an Oikos • Web and Circle of Relationships

Common

Kinship Relationships
Immediate, extended, and adopted
family members

Acquaintances & Friendships
Significant others, neighbors in proximity,
"friends of friends"

Associates & Connections
Work mates, special interests, ethnic,
national, cultural ties

Strategically
Powerful

No "Cold
Calling"

Historically
Effective

Relationally
Receptive

Biblically
Based

Entirely
Natural

Least
Threatening

Appendix 16

Paul's Team Members

Companions, Laborers, and Fellow Workers

Rev. Dr. Don L. Davis

Achaicus, a Corinthian who visited Paul at Philippi, 1 Cor. 16.17.

Archippus, Colossian disciple whom Paul exhorted to fulfill his ministry, Col. 4.17; Philem. 2.

Aquila, Jewish disciple Paul found at Corinth, Acts 18.2, 18, 26; Rom. 16.3; 1 Cor. 16.19; 2 Tim. 4.19.

Aristarchus, with Paul on 3rd journey, Acts 19.29; 20.4; 27.2; Col. 4.10; Philem. 24.

Artemas, companion of Paul at Nicopolis, Titus 3.12.

Barnabas, a Levite, cousin of John Mark, and companion with Paul in several of his journeys, cf. Acts 4.36, 9.27; 11.22, 25, 30; 12.25; chs. 13, 14, and 15; 1 Cor. 9.6; Gal. 2.1, 9, 13; Col. 4.13.

Carpus, disciple of Troas, 2 Tim. 4.13.

Claudia, female disciple of Rome, 2 Tim. 4.21.

Clement, fellow-laborer at Phillipi, Phil. 4.3.

Crescens, a disciple at Rome, 2 Tim. 4.10.

Demas, a laborer of Paul at Rome, Col. 4.14; Philem. 24; 2 Tim. 4.10.

Epaphras, fellow laborer and prisoner, Col. 1.7, 4.12; Philem. 23.

Epaphroditus, messenger between Paul and the churches, Phil. 2.25, 4.18.

Eubulus, disciple of Rome, 2 Tim. 4.21.

Euodia, Christian woman of Philippi, Phil. 4.2

Fortunatus, part of the Corinthian team, 1 Cor. 16.17.

Gaius, 1) a Macedonian companion, Acts 19.29; 2) a disciple/companion in Derbe, Acts 20.4.

Jesus (Justus), a Jewish disciple at Colossae, Col. 4.11.

John Mark, companion of Paul and cousin of Barnabas, Acts 12.12, 15; 15.37, 39; Col. 4.10; 2 Tim. 4.11; Philem. 24.

Linus, a Roman Companion of Paul, 2 Tim. 4.21.

Luke, physician and fellow-traveler with Paul, Col. 4.14; 2 Tim. 4.11; Philem. 24.

Onesimus, native of Colossae and slave of Philemon who served Paul, Col. 4.9; Philem. 10.

Hermogenes, a team member who abandoned Paul in prison, 2 Tim. 1.15.

Phygellus, one with Hermogenes turned from Paul in Asia, 2 Tim. 1.15.

Priscilla (Prisca), wife of Aquila of Pontus and fellow-worker in the Gospel, Acts 18.2, 18, 26; Rom. 16.3; 1 Cor. 16.19.

Pudens, a Roman companion of Paul, 2 Tim. 4.21.

Secundus, companion of Paul on his way from Greece to Syria, Acts 20.4.

Silas, disciple, fellow laborer, and prisoner with Paul, Acts 15.22, 27, 32, 34, 40; 16.19, 25, 29; 17.4, 10, etc.

Sopater, accompanied Paul to Syria, Acts 20.4.

Sosipater, kinsman of Paul, Rom. 16.21.

Silvanus, probably same as Silas, 2 Cor. 1.19; 1 Thess. 1.1; 2 Thess. 1.1.

Sosthenes, Chief Ruler of the Synagogue of Corinth, laborer with Paul there, Acts 18.17.

Stephanus, one of the first believers of Achaia and visitor to Paul, 1 Cor. 1.16; 16.15; 16.17.

Syntyche, one of Paul's female "fellow workers" in Philippi, Phil. 4.2.

Tertius, slave and person who wrote the Epistle to the Romans, Rom. 16.22.

Timothy, a young man of Lystra with a Jewish mother and Greek father who labored on with Paul in his ministry, Acts 16.1; 17.14, 15; 18.5; 19.22; 20.4; Rom. 16.21; 1 Cor. 4.17; 16.10; 2 Cor. 1.1, 19; Phil. 1.1; 2.19; Col. 1.1; 1 Thess. 1.1; 3.2, 6; 2 Thess. 1.1; 1 Tim. 1.2, 18; 6.20; 2 Tim. 1.2; Philem. 1; Heb. 13.23.

Titus, Greek disciple and co-laborer of Paul, 2 Cor. 2.13; 7.6, 13, 14; 8.6, 16, 23; 12.18; Gal. 2.1, 3; 2 Tim. 4.10; Titus 1.4.

Trophimus, Ephesian disciple who accompanied Paul to Jerusalem from Greece, Acts 20.4; 21.29; 2 Tim. 4.20.

Tryphena and *Tryphosa*, female disciples of Rome, probably twins, who Paul calls laborers in the Lord, Rom. 16.12.

Tychicus, a disciple of Asia Minor who accompanied Paul in various trips, Acts 20.4; Eph. 6.21; Col. 4.7; 2 Tim. 4.12; Titus 3.12.

Urbanus, Roman disciple and aid to Paul, Rom. 16.9.

Appendix 17
Getting a Firm Grasp of Scripture
From Leroy Eims, *The Lost Art of Disciple Making*, p. 81

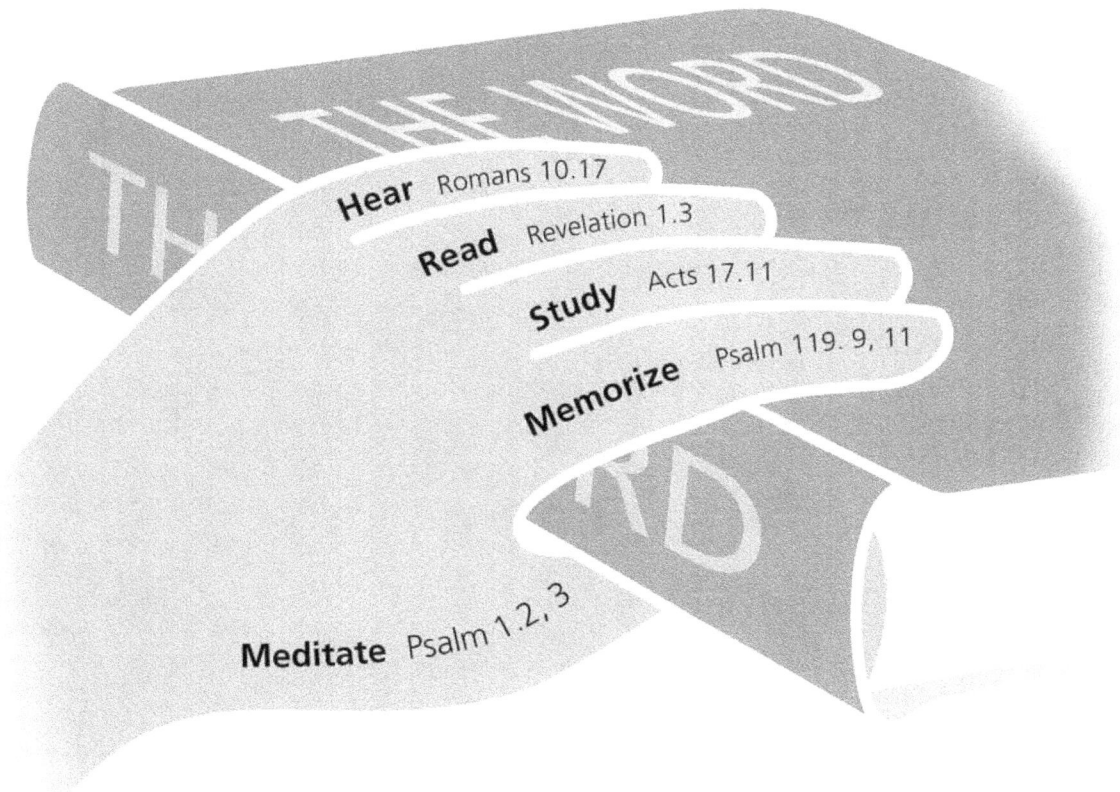

Appendix 18
Spiritual Growth Diagram
From Leroy Eims, *The Lost Art of Disciple Making*, p. 183

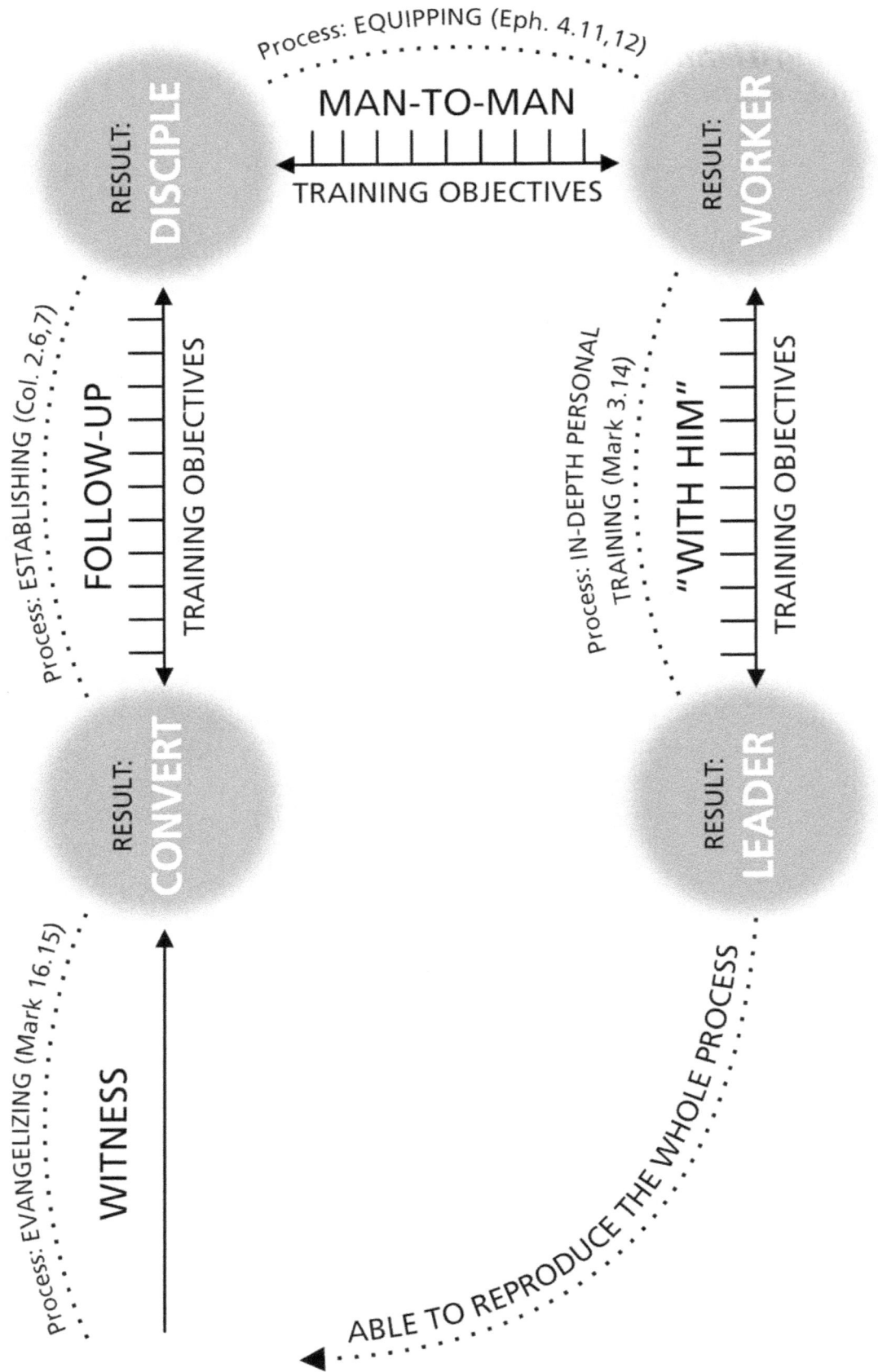

Process: EQUIPPING (Eph. 4.11,12)

MAN-TO-MAN

TRAINING OBJECTIVES

RESULT: DISCIPLE

RESULT: WORKER

FOLLOW-UP

TRAINING OBJECTIVES

Process: ESTABLISHING (Col. 2.6,7)

"WITH HIM"

TRAINING OBJECTIVES

Process: IN-DEPTH PERSONAL TRAINING (Mark 3.14)

RESULT: CONVERT

RESULT: LEADER

WITNESS

Process: EVANGELIZING (Mark 16.15)

ABLE TO REPRODUCE THE WHOLE PROCESS

Appendix 19

Personal Growth vs. Body Life: Connections

Rev. Dr. Don L. Davis

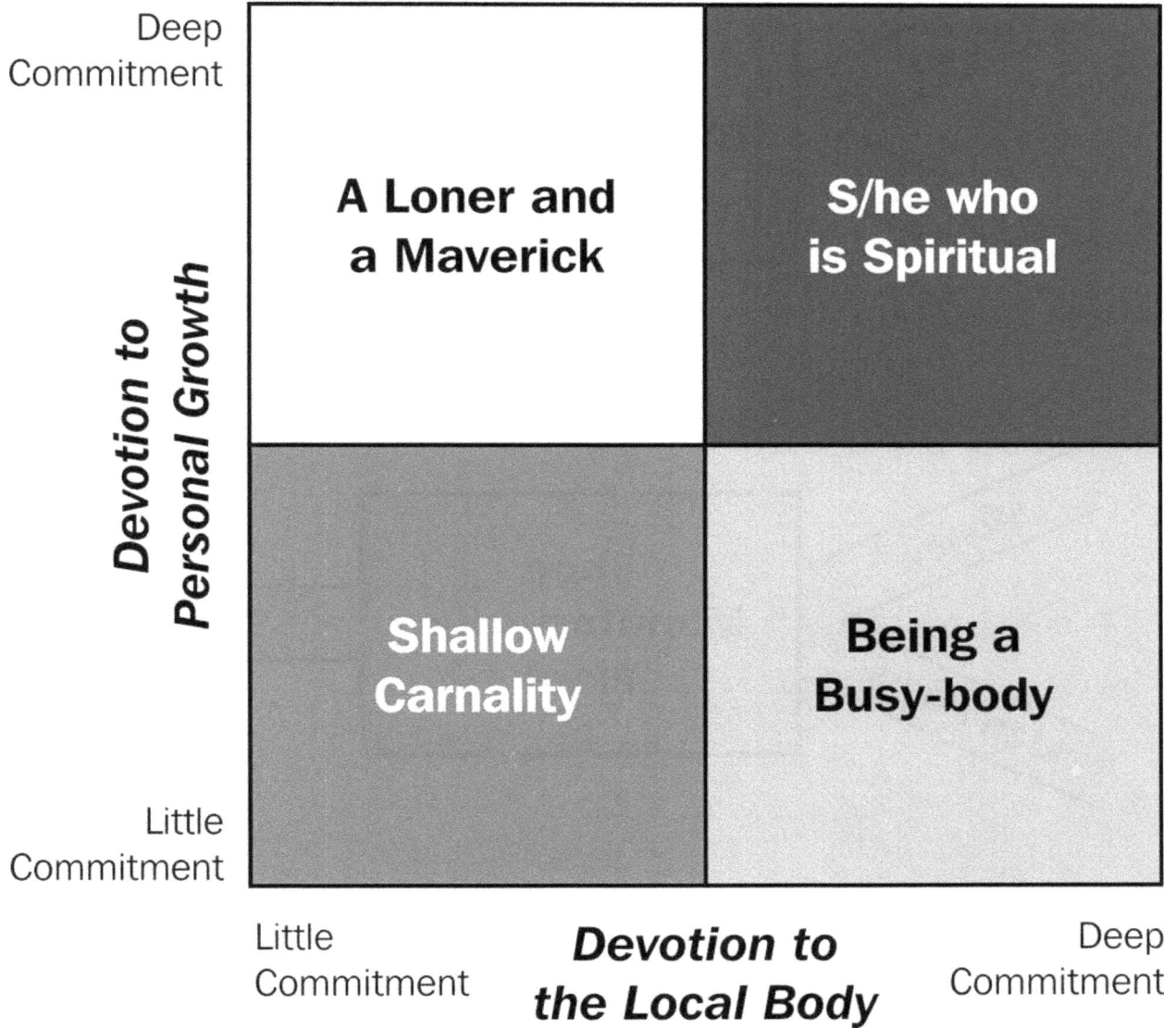

Deep
Commitment

**Devotion to
Personal Growth**

| **A Loner and a Maverick** | **S/he who is Spiritual** |
| **Shallow Carnality** | **Being a Busy-body** |

Little
Commitment

Little
Commitment

*Devotion to
the Local Body*

Deep
Commitment

Appendix 20
Shoe Manufacturing Plant
From Leroy Eims, *The Lost Art of Disciple Making*, p. 60

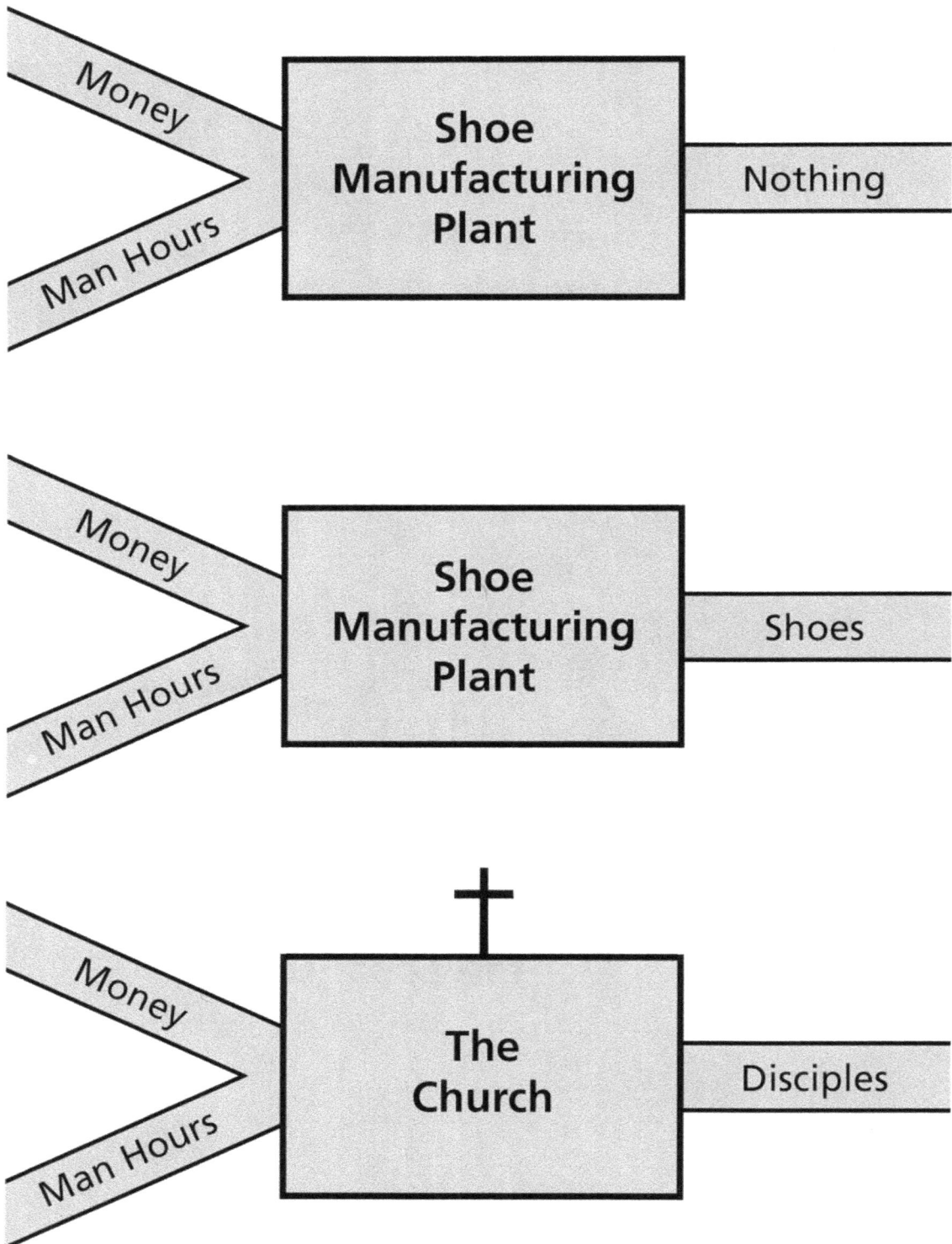

Money
Man Hours
→ **Shoe Manufacturing Plant** → Nothing

Money
Man Hours
→ **Shoe Manufacturing Plant** → Shoes

Money
Man Hours
→ **The Church** → Disciples

Appendix 21

Fit to Represent: Multiplying Disciples of the Kingdom of God

Rev. Dr. Don L. Davis

Luke 10.16 (ESV) - The one who hears you hears me, and the one who rejects you rejects me, and the one who rejects me rejects him who sent me.

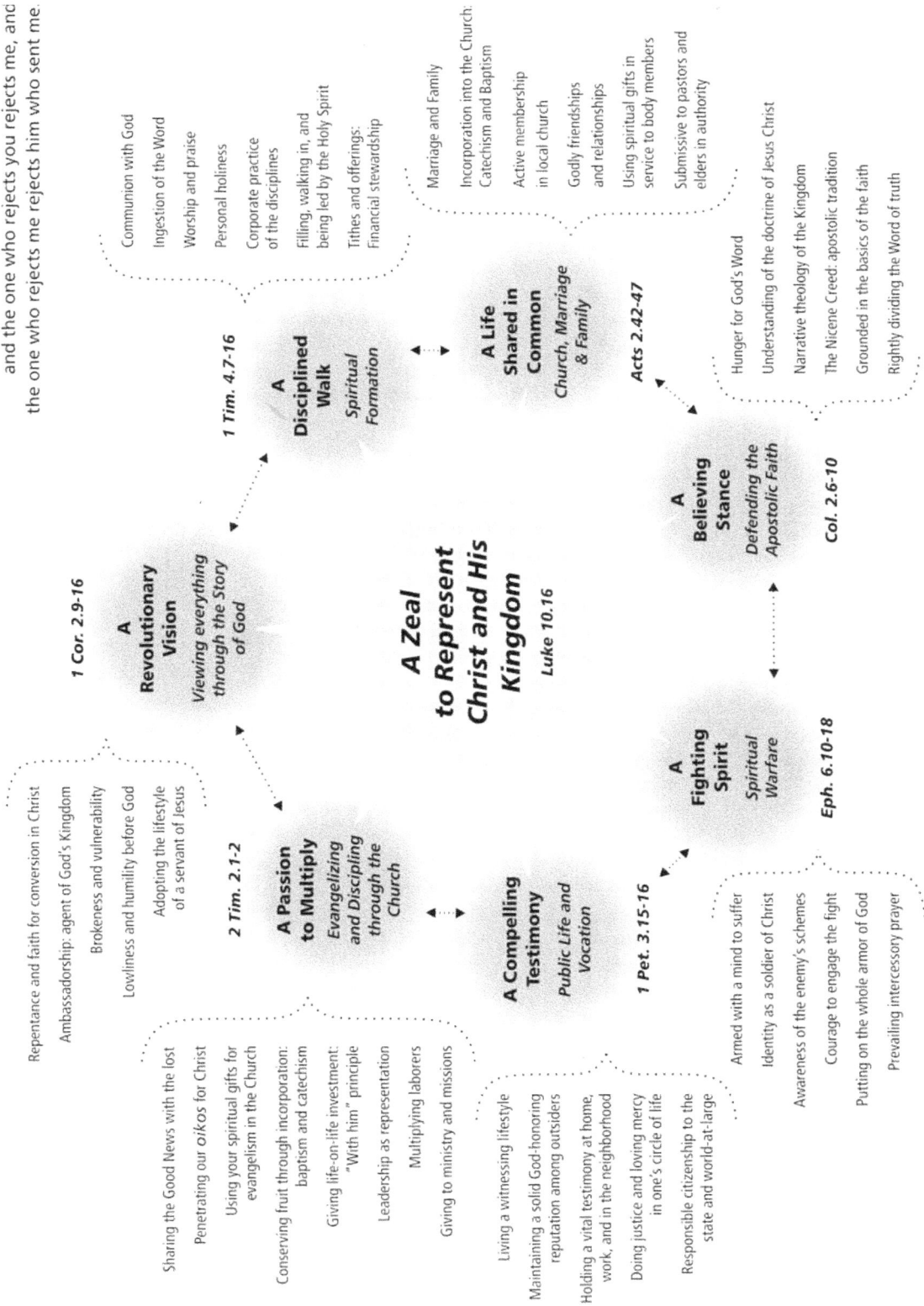

A Zeal to Represent Christ and His Kingdom
Luke 10.16

A Revolutionary Vision
Viewing everything through the Story of God
1 Cor. 2.9-16

A Disciplined Walk
Spiritual Formation
1 Tim. 4.7-16

- Communion with God
- Ingestion of the Word
- Worship and praise
- Personal holiness
- Corporate practice of the disciplines
- Filling, walking in, and being led by the Holy Spirit
- Tithes and offerings: Financial stewardship

A Life Shared in Common
Church, Marriage & Family
Acts 2.42-47

- Marriage and Family
- Incorporation into the Church: Catechism and Baptism
- Active membership in local church
- Godly friendships and relationships
- Using spiritual gifts in service to body members
- Submissive to pastors and elders in authority

A Believing Stance
Defending the Apostolic Faith
Col. 2.6-10

- Hunger for God's Word
- Understanding of the doctrine of Jesus Christ
- Narrative theology of the Kingdom
- The Nicene Creed: apostolic tradition
- Grounded in the basics of the faith
- Rightly dividing the Word of truth

A Passion to Multiply
Evangelizing and Discipling through the Church
2 Tim. 2.1-2

- Repentance and faith for conversion in Christ
- Ambassadorship: agent of God's Kingdom
- Brokeness and vulnerability
- Lowliness and humility before God
- Adopting the lifestyle of a servant of Jesus

- Sharing the Good News with the lost
- Penetrating our *oikos* for Christ
- Using your spiritual gifts for evangelism in the Church
- Conserving fruit through incorporation: baptism and catechism
- Giving life-on-life investment: "With him" principle
- Leadership as representation
- Multiplying laborers
- Giving to ministry and missions

A Compelling Testimony
Public Life and Vocation
1 Pet. 3.15-16

- Living a witnessing lifestyle
- Maintaining a solid God-honoring reputation among outsiders
- Holding a vital testimony at home, work, and in the neighborhood
- Doing justice and loving mercy in one's circle of life
- Responsible citizenship to the state and world-at-large

A Fighting Spirit
Spiritual Warfare
Eph. 6.10-18

- Armed with a mind to suffer
- Identity as a soldier of Christ
- Awareness of the enemy's schemes
- Courage to engage the fight
- Putting on the whole armor of God
- Prevailing intercessory prayer

Appendix 22

From Deep Ignorance to Credible Witness

Rev. Dr. Don L. Davis

Witness - Ability to give witness and teach 2 Tim. 2.2 Matt. 28.18-20 1 John 1.1-4 Prov. 20.6 2 Cor. 5.18-21	*And the things you have heard me say in the presence of many witnesses entrust to reliable men who will also be qualified to teach others.* *~ 2 Tim. 2.2* **8**
Lifestyle - Consistent appropriation and habitual practice based on beliefs Heb. 5.11-6.2 Eph. 4.11-16 2 Pet. 3.18 1 Tim. 4.7-10	*And Jesus increased in wisdom and in stature, and in favor with God and man.* *~ Luke 2.52* **7**
Demonstration - Expressing conviction in corresponding conduct, speech, and behavior James 2.14-26 2 Cor. 4.13 2 Pet. 1.5-9 1 Thess. 1.3-10	*Nevertheless, at your word I will let down the net.* *~ Luke 5.5* **6**
Conviction - Committing oneself to think, speak, and act in light of information Heb. 2.3-4 Heb. 11.1, 6 Heb. 3.15-19 Heb. 4.2-6	*Do you believe this?* *~ John 11.26* **5**
Discernment - Understanding the meaning and implications of information John 16.13 Eph. 1.15-18 Col. 1.9-10 Isa. 6.10; 29.10	*Do you understand what you are reading?* *~ Acts 8.30* **4**
Knowledge - Ability to recall and recite information 2 Tim. 3.16-17 1 Cor. 2.9-16 1 John 2.20-27 John 14.26	*For what does the Scripture say?* *~ Rom. 4.3* **3**
Interest - Responding to ideas or information with both curiosity and openness Ps. 42.1-2 Acts 9.4-5 John 12.21 1 Sam. 3.4-10	*We will hear you again on this matter.* *~ Acts 17.32* **2**
Awareness - General exposure to ideas and information Mark 7.6-8 Acts 19.1-7 John 5.39-40 Matt. 7.21-23	*At that time, Herod the tetrarch heard about the fame of Jesus.* *~ Matt. 14.1* **1**
Ignorance - Unfamiliarity with information due to naivete, indifference, or hardness Eph. 4.17-19 Ps. 2.1-3 Rom. 1.21; 2.19 1 John 2.11	*Who is the Lord that I should heed his voice?* *~ Exod. 5.2* **0**

Appendix 23

Laws of Sowing and Reaping

Rev. Dr. Don L. Davis

The Laws of Sowing and Reaping: Personal Discipline and Fruitfulness	
The Law	**The Explanation**
You will reap what you sow	Sow to the Spirit and reap God's best
You will reap what others have sown	Transcend the harvest you have inherited
You reap the same in kind as what you sow	Choose wisely what you want to reap before you sow
You reap in proportion to what you sow	Sow more to get more in return
You reap in a different season than when you sow	Learn to be patient as you await the harvest
You reap more than what you sow	It is going to be better (or worse) than you gave
You can always transcend last year's harvest	God gives the growth, so trust in him alone

We cannot help but see that the [people] who have achieved wonders in modern science and technology are [people] of very great inner discipline. No one has succeeded by following the path of least resistance.

~ Elton Trueblood. *The Yoke of Christ*.
Waco, TX: Word Books, 1958. p. 128.

Prayer and Affirmation to God

Do not be deceived: God is not mocked, for whatever one sows, that will he also reap. [8] For the one who sows to his own flesh will from the flesh reap corruption, but the one who sows to the Spirit will from the Spirit reap eternal life. [9] And let us not grow weary of doing good, for in due season we will reap, if we do not give up.

~ Galatians 6.7-9

Appendix 24
Roles of Effective Discipling
Rev. Dr. Don L. Davis

	Model	*Mentor*	*Friend*
Scriptural Reference	1 Cor. 11.1	Phil 4.9	John 15.15
Central Picture	Example	Coach	Comrade
Primary Duty	Set the Pace	Provide Advice	Share the Journey
Rubber on the Road	Your Walk	Your Talk	Your Heart
Key Goal	Inspire	Instruct	Infect

Appendix 25
The Power of Multiplication
2 Timothy 2.2 Discipleship Diagram
Rev. Dr. Don L. Davis

Paul

Timothy And Many Witnesses

The Same Commit Thou To Faithful Men

Who Shall Be Able To Teach Others Also

2 Tim. 2.2 (ESV) - And what you have heard from me in the presence of many witnesses entrust to faithful men who will be able to teach others also.

Appendix 26
The Hump
Rev. Dr. Don L. Davis

The Baby Christian
The New Believer and the Spiritual Disciplines

Awkwardness

Unskillfulness

Mistakes

Roughness

Sporadic Behavior

Uncomfortableness

Inefficiency

Novice-Level Performance

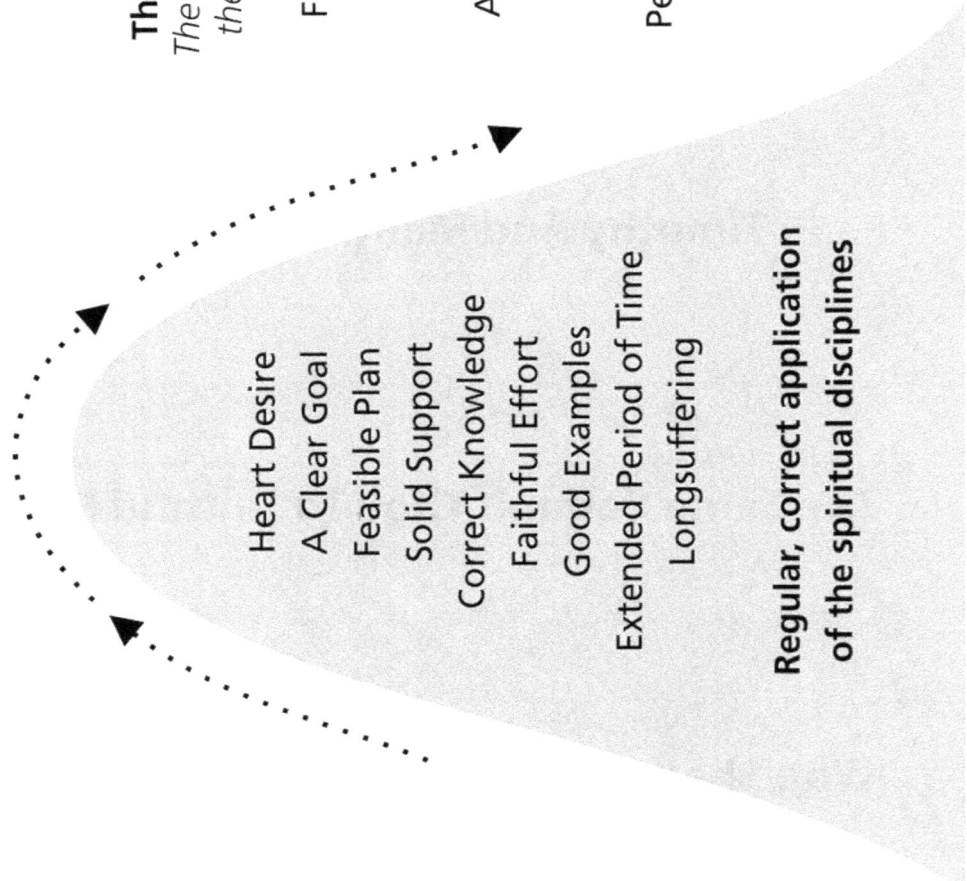

The Mature Christian
The Mature Believer and the Spiritual Disciplines

Faithful Application

Gracefulness

Automatic response

Comfortableness

Personal Satisfaction

Excellence

Expertise

Training Others

Heart Desire
A Clear Goal
Feasible Plan
Solid Support
Correct Knowledge
Faithful Effort
Good Examples
Extended Period of Time
Longsuffering

Regular, correct application of the spiritual disciplines

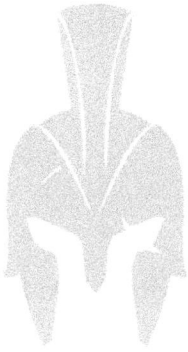

Appendix 27

Principles of Spiritual Growth

Rev. Dr. Don L. Davis

1. Spirituality is first concerned with the realm of the spirit, especially to the Holy Spirit, and then through what we know, believe, feel, and choose as individuals and in relationship with others (1 Cor. 2.9-16).

2. Spirituality is not perceived firsthand, but is rather revealed through the words, conduct, and actions of our personal lives (Matt. 7.15-20; 12.33-37).

3. Spirituality is fundamentally concerned with the shaping of one's life vision – how we interpret and evaluate reality. The perceptions we form, believe in, and rely on in our minds and spirits help to cause our emotions, determine our decisions, affect our behavior, and circumscribe our relationships (John 8.31-32; Heb. 11.6).

4. To grow up in Christ, then, is to know and walk boldly in the mind of Christ, directing our personal growth efforts toward becoming more aware of our personal vision, challenging the lies that contradict his Word, and speak and act consistently with what Scripture affirms and denies (2 Tim. 3.16-17; 2 Cor. 10.3-5).

Areas of Spiritual Vision

- The Way Things WERE

- The Way Things ARE

- The Way Things WILL BE

- The MEANING and VALUE of Things

- The Way Things SHOULD BE

The Areas of Ultimate Concern

Self – Others – Life – World – God

Appendix 28
A Spiritual Warfare Bibliography
Rev. Dr. Don L. Davis

Anderson, Dr. Neil T. *Released from Bondage*. San Bernardino, CA: Here's Life Publishers, 1991.

——. *The Bondage Breaker*. Eugene, OR: Harvest House Publishers, 1993.

Arn, Win and Charles Arn. *The Master's Plan for Making Disciples*. 2nd Ed. Grand Rapids: Baker Book House, 1998.

Billheimer, Paul. *Destined for the Throne*. Minneapolis: Bethany House, 1975.

——. *Destined to Overcome*. Minneapolis: Bethany House Publishers, 1982.

Eims, Leroy. *The Lost Art of Disciple Making*. Grand Rapids, MI: Zondervan Publishing House, 1978.

Epp, Theodore H. *The Believer's Spiritual Warfare*. Lincoln: Back to the Bible, 1973.

Dawson, John. *Taking Our Cities for God*. Lake Mary, FL: Creation House, 1989.

Grounds, Vernon. *Radical Commitment: Getting Serious about Christian Growth*. Portland, OR: Multnomah Press, 1984.

Hayford, Jack. *Answering the Call to Evangelism* (*Spirit Filled Life Kingdom Dynamics Study Guides*). Nashville: Thomas Nelson Publishers, 1995.

Holly, James L. M.D. *The Basis of Victory in Spiritual Warfare: The Blood of Jesus Christ*. Beaumont, TX: Mission and Ministry to Men, Inc, 1992.

Ladd, George Eldon. *The Gospel of the Kingdom*. Grand Rapids: Eerdmans, 1999.

MacArther, John Jr. *The Believer's Armor*. Chicago, IL: Moody Press, 1986.

McAlpine, Thomas H. *Facing the Powers: What are the Options?* Eugene, OR: Wipf and Stock Publishers, 2003.

Murphy, Ed. *The Handbook for Spiritual Warfare*. Revised and updated. Nashville: Thomas Nelson Publishers, 2003.

Ortiz, Juan Carlos. *Disciple*. Carol Stream, IL: Creation House, 1982.

Phillips, Keith. *Out of Ashes*. Los Angeles: World Impact Press, 1996.

Pirolo, Neal and Yvonne. *Prepare for Battle: Basic Training in Spiritual Warfare*. San Diego, CA: Emmaus Road, International, 1997.

Shenk, David W. and Ervin R. Stutzman. *Creating Communities of the Kingdom*. Scottsdale, PA: Herald Press, 1998.

Snyder, Howard A. *Kingdom, Church, and World*. Eugene, OR: Wipf and Stock Publishers, 1985.

Stedman, Ray C. *Spiritual Warfare*. Waco, TX: Word Books, 1975.

Stratford, Lauren. *Satan's Underground*. Eugene, OR: Harvest House Publishers, 1988

Tippit, Sammy. *Fit for Battle: The Character, Weapons, and Strategies of the Spiritual Warrior*. Chicago, IL: Moody Press, 1994.

Trask, Thomas E. and Wayde I. Goodall. *The Battle: Defeating the Enemies of Your Soul*. Grand Rapids, MI: Zondervan Publishing House, 1997.

Warner, Timothy M. *Spiritual Warfare: Victory over the Powers of This Dark World*. Wheaton: Crossway Books, 1991.

White, Thomas B. *The Believer's Guide to Spiritual Warfare*. Ann Arbor, MI: Servant Publications, 1990.